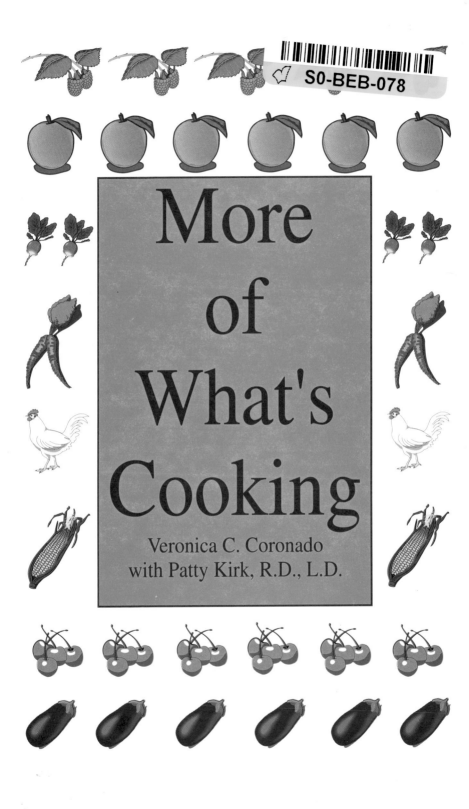

More of What's Cooking

Veronica C. Coronado
with Patty Kirk, R.D., L.D.

JUMBO JACK'S COOKBOOKS
AUDUBON MEDIA CORPORATION
301 BROADWAY • AUDUBON IA 50025
1-800-798-2635

First Printing - December 1995

Second Printing - March 1996

Published by Apples to Zucchini, Inc.

Cover designed with *Corel Draw!* software.

ISBN 0-9649658-0-1

Order blanks are included in back of book
for your convenience.

Dedication

To my husband Chuck, whose loving
support and mutual enjoyment of
cooking, made this cookbook a reality.

To the Lord, enabler, encourager, provider.

Acknowledgments

Jalaine
Mackinnon
Nancy Smith
Penny Hollyfield

Barbara
Costello

Edna
Ground
Carole Kerby
John Baer

Charles Coronado
Maureen Reynolds
Kathleen Stewart
Reagan Stewart
Jo Nell Stewart

Many thanks to
the friends and family
who have shared their
recipes and time to make
this cookbook
possible

Assistant Editor
Courtney Hollyfield

Photographer
Kevin Costello

As a nutrition data analyst, Veronica Coronado has assisted many individuals, corporations, health facilities, and restaurants with nutritional analysis of eating plans and recipes. Veronica has consulted with The Dallas Morning News, analyzing recipes featured in their weekly food section. Others that she has consulted with include American Airlines, la Madeleine, American Heart Association, The Greenhouse, Conoco, and Natura Cafe. She has helped many authors, analyzing recipes for their books, including Kenneth H. Cooper, M.D., M.P.H. (Kid Fitness) and Renie Steves (Fort Worth is Cooking!).

Veronica co-authored What's Cooking at the Cooper Clinic and makes frequent appearances promoting the cookbook and demonstrating low-fat cooking.

Veronica earned a B.S. in Nutrition from the University of Texas at Austin in 1985. She currently resides in Dallas with her husband and cooking companion, Charles Coronado.

As a registered and licensed dietitian, Patty Kirk spends her time counseling patients for weight management, cardiovascular nutrition, and the development of healthier lifestyles through healthy eating. Patty teaches nutrition and weight management classes to corporations and community groups and has coordinated such printed educational materials as Eating on the Run, Eating Out, Fast Food Choices, and Healthy Eating and Weight Control. She also gives numerous cooking demonstrations illustrating the art of incorporating flavorful and healthy choices in the kitchen.

Patty earned her degree in Nutrition from Kansas State University and interned with Parkland Hospital in conjunction with The University of Texas Health Science Center in Dallas, Texas. Patty currently resides in Dallas with her husband, Rich Kirk, and two daughters, Ashley and Amanda Kirk.

V

Contents

Introduction

Three years prior to the publication of the first cookbook I co-authored, *What's Cooking at the Cooper Clinic*, I perceived the need for a low-fat cookbook that included easy, no-fuss recipes. This first cookbook was initially intended to be used as a tool by Cooper Clinic patients; however, when the public learned of the forthcoming cookbook, there was an immediate demand for such a collection of recipes. Before I knew it, we had requests to have it in the bookstores. And so it went, to patients, to the bookstores, to garden club talks, to Canada...

The greatest feeling of achievement came when patients, friends, and cookbook customers from all areas of the country would tell me success stories. One such story tells of how a husband lost 15 pounds in 1 month, just by cooking out of the book. Such accolades as, "Made your Chicken Bow Tie Pasta last night, loved it!" and "I cook out of your book every night!" filled my office daily. The compliments the recipes received highlighted the simplicity of preparation, the easy-to-find ingredients, the great presentation, but most of all, the great taste!

And so I bring you *More of What's Cooking*, a collection of heart-healthy, fun-to-make recipes that you, your family, and friends are sure to enjoy. You will find the same simplicity of preparation, easy-to-find ingredients, great presentation, and more wonderful great tastes. You will be enticed by the use of fresh herbs, notes to you about either serving suggestions, significant nutrients, or why we like the recipe. There are simpler vegetables, more fruit-packed desserts, and use of such newer products on the market as balsamic vinegar, sun-dried tomatoes, and light cake mixes.

Whether you are a novice cook or seasoned entertainer, I hope you find great enjoyment in making healthier cooking part of your lifestyle.

Veronica Coronado

Some Reasons to Cook

Cooking healthy at home is one giant step towards **healthy living**.

The **smell** of something cooking makes a house feel like home.

Memories are created around food, and just the smell of Mom's dish, or Grandmother's pie can bring a rush of wonderful memories.

Cooking can be **fun**!

If you consider cooking to be a chore, try one of these ideas to find enjoyment in cooking.

Choose just one new food to make for dinner, for example, the Beef in Shallot Sauce. Complement it with a baked potato and steamed broccoli and you have a great meal with little fuss.

Invest in good cooking utensils. A garlic press that really does the job is worth the few extra dollars to save hassle. Buy one good quality knife as opposed to a whole set. You will appreciate how much quicker and easier cutting up vegetables will be. Later you can invest in more knives.

Cook for a friend, elderly family member or single neighbor. Nothing is more encouraging to a cook than sharing a portion of your homemade fare with someone who normally eats frozen dinners alone. Likewise, brighten a sick friend's day with a container of soup; whether you made it fresh or had it frozen from weeks before, it will be appreciated.

Form a supper club where the host makes the entree and guests bring the side dishes and dessert. A sure way to enjoy a delicious meal and warm company; not to mention recipes and cooking secrets!

Try something new, a new method of cooking or a new ingredient.

Attend a cooking class. The number of classes offered in Dallas each week is astounding. Listed in the Food Section of the Dallas Morning News, you can learn anything from Italian cooking to bread baking. Check your local newspaper for class schedules.

About the Nutrition Analysis

Each recipe has been analyzed using either Key Home Gourmet or Cooper Clinic Nutrition and Exercise Evaluation System.

A few points to note:

• The analysis includes all recipe ingredients listed prior to the instructions. Those ingredients listed as optional are not included in the analysis.

• When a choice of ingredients is listed, the first ingredient is the one included in the analysis.

• When a range is given for an ingredient (1 to 1 1/2 cups flour), the average of the two amounts is used (1 1/4 cups).

• When a recipe includes a marinade, only the portion of the marinade ingredients that remain after draining are included in the analysis.

• Spices are dried unless fresh ones are specified.

All recipes have been modified to be reduced in fat, cholesterol, and sodium. For those individuals with hypertension, further modifications can be made by deleting salt and using unsalted products when available. For further fat reduction, substitute fat-free products for reduced-fat or light products.

Abbreviations

c.	-	cup	oz.	-	ounce
cal	-	calorie	pro	-	protein
carb	-	carbohydrate	pt.	-	pint
chol	-	cholesterol	qt.	-	quart
gm	-	gram	T.	-	tablespoon
lb.	-	pound	tsp.	-	teaspoon
mg	-	milligram			

Tips for making your favorite recipe healthier

A quick glance at the common sources of fat in a recipe:

Ingredient:	Fat/Measurement:
bacon	10 gm / 1 slice raw, 3 gm / 1 slice cooked
cheese	9 gm / ounce or 1/4 cup shredded
cottage cheese	10 gm / cup
cream cheese	5 gm / tablespoon
cream soup	20 gm / 10 3/4 ounce can
eggs	5 gm / egg
half & half	28 gm / cup
margarine & butter	11 gm / tablespoon
mayonnaise	11 gm / tablespoon
milk, whole	8 gm / cup
oils	13 to 14 gm / tablespoon
salad dressings	7 to 9 gm / tablespoon
sour cream	48 gm / cup
whipping cream	88 gm / cup

A look at the fat in "lighter" products:

Ingredient:	Fat/measurement:
Canadian bacon	2 gm / ounce
cheese, low-fat	3 gm / ounce or 1/4 cup shredded
cheese, reduced-fat	5 gm / ounce or 1/4 cup shredded
cottage cheese, 1%	2 gm / cup
cream cheese, 30% less fat	3 gm / tablespoon
cream soup, reduced-fat & sodium	7.5gm / 10 3/4 ounce can
egg whites or egg substitute	0 gm / 2 egg whites or 1/4 cup egg substitute
margarine, light	5 to 6 gm / tablespoon
mayonnaise, light	5 gm / tablespoon
salad dressings, reduced-calorie	1 to 3 gm / tablespoon
skim milk	0 to 1 gm / cup
sour cream, light	20 gm / cup

1 cup = 16 tablespoons

- Start with the oil. Reduce it in half or more. If the recipe makes 4 main dish servings, decrease the oil to 1 to 1 1/2 tablespoons.

- If there is cheese, use low-fat or reduced-fat cheese and try half as much.

- Replace whipping cream with equal portions of skim milk and half & half. Or try evaporated skim milk instead of whipping cream. For example, replace 1 cup whipping cream with 1/2 cup skim milk and 1/2 cup half & half or 1 cup evaporated skim milk. If using the skim milk/half & half substitution, reduce fat further by using 1/4 cup each.

- When making muffins, decrease oil or margarine to 2 to 4 tablespoons or omit it all together. If desired, replace oil and margarine with an equivalent amount of unsweetened applesauce.

- Replace mayonnaise with half fat-free mayonnaise and half light mayonnaise to get the "mayo" taste. To further decrease the fat, cut back on the amount of this mayonnaise combination.

- Replace eggs with egg whites or egg substitute, using 2 egg whites or 1/4 cup egg substitute for 1 egg.

- Substitute light or fat-free products for their regular counterparts, i.e. sour cream, cottage cheese, cake mixes, yogurts, etc.

- Replace whole milk with skim milk.

- Reduce nuts to 2 to 4 tablespoons per recipe.

A sample of a favorite recipe made healthier

Strawberry Cake

Lower-fat version:
no oil
5 oz. plus 3 T, sweetened frozen strawberries, divided use
1 (18 1/4 oz.) box light white cake mix
1 (3 oz.) box strawberry gelatin
1 T. flour
1 1/2 c. water
1 c. egg substitute or 8 egg whites
Nonstick vegetable cooking spray
2 1/2 c. powdered sugar
1/4 tsp. salt
6 T. margarine, softened

Original version:
1 c. vegetable oil
5 oz. plus 3 T. sweetened frozen strawberries, divided use
Regular cake mix

1 (3 oz.) box strawberry gelatin
1 T. flour
1/2 c. water*
4 eggs
Nonstick vegetable cooking spray
2 1/2 c. powdered sugar
1/4 tsp. salt
8 T. margarine, softened

*Because of the gelatin in this recipe, we increased the water to replace the liquid lost in deleting the oil in the original recipe.

Yield: 20 servings
Per Serving Lower-fat Version:
   229 cal, 6 gm fat, 2 gm pro, 42 gm carb, 0 mg chol, 266 mg sodium, 0 gm dietary fiber

Yield: 20 servings
Per Serving Original Version:
   345 cal, 19 gm fat, 3 gm pro, 41 gm carb, 43 mg chol, 275 mg sodium, 0 gm dietary fiber

For the whole cake, 2320 calories and 266 grams of fat have been saved, using these simple substitutions.

Menus
for
Healthy Entertaining

To decrease calories in these menus, skip the dessert or substitute fresh fruit

Valentines Dinner

Raspberry Chicken
(184 cal, 6 gm fat)

Blue Cheese Scalloped Potatoes
(205 cal, 5 gm fat)

Steamed Broccoli
(27 cal, 0 gm fat)

Strawberry Chocolate Chip Shortcake
Make heart-shaped shortcakes
(228 cal, 7 gm fat)

Menu Total
644 cal, 18 gm fat

Italian Buffet

Bruschetta with Roasted Garlic and Parmesan Cheese
(110 cal, 3 gm fat)

Red and Green Pasta
(397 cal, 8 gm fat)

White Lasagna with Canadian Bacon
(232 cal, 5 gm fat)

Asparagus with Parmesan Cheese
(30 cal, 1 gm fat)

Red Peppered Yellow Squash
(34 cal, 1 gm fat)

Chocolate Chip Biscotti
(100 cal, 2 gm fat)

Menu Total
(With half portion of each entree and vegetable)
557 cal, 13 gm fat

Spring Picnic

Turkey Muffuletta with Tomato Pesto
(270 cal, 7 gm fat)

Asparagus Salad
(42 cal, 3 gm fat)

Black Bean Pasta Salad
(126 cal, 2 gm fat)

Berry Patch Bars
(90 cal, 2 gm fat)

Menu Total
528 cal, 14 gm fat

Easter Brunch

Field Salad with Strawberries and Jicama
(66 cal, 3 gm fat)

Spinach Quiche
(219 cal, 9 gm fat)

Cherry and Orange Scones
(158 cal, 4 gm fat)

Flowered Angel Food Cake
(199 cal, 2 gm fat)

Menu Total
642 cal, 18 gm fat

Fourth of July Breakfast Buffet

Hash Brown Casserole
(198 cal, 5 gm fat)

Fresh Fruit Salad
(90 cal, 0 gm fat)

Blueberry Sour Cream Coffeecake
(208 cal, 5 gm fat)

Stawberry Cornmeal Muffins
(147 cal, 2 gm fat)

Nonfat, Sugar-free Yogurts
(100 cal, 0 gm fat)

Guests choose their favorites.

South of the Border

Shrimp Enchiladas
(297 cal, 9 gm fat)

Refried Black Beans
(114 cal, <1 gm fat)

Chocolate Pound Cake with Mexican-Chocolate Glaze
(238 cal, 6 gm fat)

Menu Total
649 cal, 15 gm fat

Autumn Dinner for Friends

Herb-Roasted Chicken and Potatoes
(311 cal, 9 gm fat)

Lemon Thyme Green Beans
(43 cal, 0 gm fat)

Orange-Glazed Carrots
(81 cal, 0 gm fat)

Dutch Apple Crumble
(249 cal, 6 gm fat)

Menu Total
684 cal, 15 gm fat

A Holiday Gathering of Friends

Southern Salad
(163 cal, 6 gm fat)

Pork Tenderloin with Dijon Mustard Sauce
(196 cal, 8 gm fat)

Corn Casserole
(138 cal, 1 gm fat)

Raspberry Carrots
(77 cal, 2 gm fat)

Menu Total
574 cal, 17 gm fat

Beverages

Iced Cappuccino
Root Beer Float
Vanilla Milkshake
Peach and Strawberry Smoothy
Banana Smoothy
Frozen Lemonade
Frozen Cherry Limeade
Cran-Raspberry Spritzer
Peach Spritzer
Orange Spritzer
Sangria Spritzer
Christmas Cranberry Cider
Spiced Warmer

Iced Cappuccino

We call this the adult milkshake. So refreshing!

1/2 c. cold, brewed espresso coffee or other coffee brewed
　　double strength
3/4 c. skim milk
1/2 c. flavored, fat-free coffee creamer (Kahlua, Amaretto, etc.)
14 (about 3 c.) ice cubes
2 tsp. chocolate sprinkles

1.　Pour coffee, milk and creamer into blender. Add 1/2 the ice
　　cubes and process until large ice chunks are gone. Add remain-
　　ing ice cubes and process until smooth.
2.　Pour into 2 tall glasses and top each with 1 teaspoon chocolate
　　sprinkles.

Yield: 2 servings
Per Serving:
　　170 cal, 0 gm fat, 3 gm pro, 37 gm carb, 2 mg chol,
　　68 mg sodium, 0 gm dietary fiber

Root Beer Float

Serve this in tall ice cream soda glasses to capture that "old-fashioned" feeling.

1 c. light vanilla ice cream
12 oz. diet root beer

1.　In 2 tall glasses place 1/2 cup ice cream each.
2.　Pour 6 ounces root beer over each and enjoy.

Yield: 2 servings
Per Serving:
　　100 cal, 2 gm fat, 3 gm pro, 17 gm carb, 10 mg chol,
　　99 mg sodium, 0 gm dietary fiber

Vanilla Milkshake

For a variation, use chocolate, strawberry or your favorite ice cream flavor.

1 c. light vanilla ice cream
1/2 c. skim milk
1/2 tsp. vanilla extract

1. Place all ingredients in blender and process until smooth.
2. Pour into a tall glass.

Yield: 1 serving
Per Serving:
    253 cal, 4 gm fat, 10 gm pro, 41 gm carb, 22 mg chol,
    203 mg sodium, 0 gm dietary fiber

Peach and Strawberry Smoothy

A great replacement for your morning glass of juice, works well with most any combination of fruit. Beware of certain fruit combinations that can cause the smoothy to turn brown.

1 c. sliced peaches
1/2 c. strawberries, stems removed
1/4 c. orange juice

1. Place all ingredients in blender and process until smooth.

Yield: 1 serving
Per Serving:
    130 cal, 0 gm fat, 2 gm pro, 31 gm carb, 0 mg chol,
    1 mg sodium, 5 gm dietary fiber

Banana Smoothy

The addition of the pineapple-orange-banana juice really accentuates the banana flavor. This smoothy is a good source of vitamin C.

2 bananas
1/2 c. pineapple-orange-banana juice
1/4 c. nonfat sugar-free vanilla yogurt
8 ice cubes

1. Place all ingredients in blender and process until smooth.

Yield: 2 servings
Per Serving:
    148 cal, 0 gm fat, 3 gm pro, 36 gm carb, 0 mg chol,
    19 mg sodium, 2 gm dietary fiber

Frozen Lemonade

A familiar favorite without the abundance of sugar.

3 T. sugar
1/3 c. hot water
1/2 c. fresh-squeezed lemon juice
14 (about 3 c.) ice cubes
Lemon slices or fresh mint leaves (optional)

1. Combine sugar and hot water, stirring until sugar is dissolved; place in refrigerator to cool.
2. Place sugar water, lemon juice and 1/2 the ice cubes in a blender. Process until large ice chunks are gone. Add remaining ice cubes and process until smooth.
3. Pour into 2 tall glasses and top with a lemon slice or mint leaf if desired.

Yield: 2 servings
Per Serving:
    88 cal, 0 gm fat, 0 gm pro, 22 gm carb, 0 mg chol,
    0 mg sodium, 0 gm dietary fiber

Frozen Cherry Limeade

This frozen concoction recalls memories of those icy treats at the neighborhood soda-fountain.

3 T. sugar
1/3 c. hot water
1/2 c. fresh-squeezed lime juice
1/2 c. fresh or jarred cherries
14 (about 3 c.) ice cubes

1. Combine sugar and hot water, stirring until sugar is dissolved; place in refrigerator to cool.
2. Place sugar water, lime juice, cherries and 1/2 the ice cubes in a blender. Process until large ice chunks are gone. Add remaining ice cubes and process until smooth.
3. Pour into 2 tall glasses and enjoy.

Yield: 2 servings
Per Serving:
107 cal, 0 gm fat, 1 gm pro, 28 gm carb, 0 mg chol,
1 mg sodium, 1 gm dietary fiber

Spritzers

Diet ginger ale, Sprite, 7-Up or your favorite sparkling water added to any fruit juice or combination of juices offers many new options for party punch or a refreshing reduced-calorie drink sure to Spritz-up your day! Enjoy the following over ice.

Cran-Raspberry Spritzer

1/2 c. reduced-calorie cran-raspberry juice
1/2 c. diet ginger ale, Sprite or 7-Up

Yield: 1 serving
Per Serving:
     25 cal, 0 gm fat, 0 gm pro, 7 gm carb, 0 mg chol,
     36 mg sodium, 0 gm dietary fiber

Peach Spritzer

1/2 c. peach nectar
1/2 c. diet ginger ale, Sprite or 7-Up

Yield: 1 serving
Per Serving:
     67 cal, 0 gm fat, 0 gm pro, 18 gm carb, 0 mg chol,
     28 mg sodium, 0 gm dietary fiber

Orange Spritzer

1/2 c. orange juice
1/2 c. diet ginger ale, Sprite or 7-Up

Yield: 1 serving
Per Serving:
     56 cal, 0 gm fat, 1 gm pro, 13 gm carb, 0 mg chol,
     20 mg sodium, 0 gm dietary fiber

Sangria Spritzer

2 c. grape juice
1/4 c. orange juice
3 T. lime juice
3 T. lemon juice
1 1/2 c. diet ginger ale
Fresh orange, lime or lemon slices (optional)

1. Combine juices and chill.
2. Just before serving, add ginger ale. Serve over ice with fresh
    fruit slice.

Yield: 4 servings
Per Serving (1 cup):
    90 cal, 0 gm fat, 1 gm pro, 22 gm carb, 0 mg chol,
    18 mg sodium, 0 gm dietary fiber

Christmas Cranberry Cider

48 oz. reduced-calorie cranberry juice
48 oz. apple cider
1 T. mulling spice*

*Mulling spice is a combination of whole cloves, whole allspice,
cinnamon stick pieces, and dried orange peel. It is available in the
spice section of your grocery store or use the Mulling Spice recipe
in this book.

1. Place juice and cider in a slow-cooker.
2. Place mulling spices in a tea infuser or tie in a piece of cheese-
    cloth. Place in slow-cooker with juice and cider; heat on high
    for 2 1/2 to 3 hours. Serve hot.

Yield: 18 servings
Per Serving (2/3 cup):
    50 cal, 0 gm fat, 0 gm pro, 12 gm carb, 0 mg chol,
    5 mg sodium, 0 gm dietary fiber

Spiced Warmer

64 oz. apple cider
2 c. orange juice
1/2 c. lemon juice
1 1/2 c. pineapple juice
1/2 c. sugar
2 cinnamon sticks
1 tsp. whole cloves

1. Place all ingredients in a slow-cooker and heat on high for 2 1/2 to 3 hours.
2. Remove cinnamon sticks and cloves and serve hot.

Yield: 18 servings
Per Serving (2/3 cup):
    95 cal, 0 gm fat, 0 gm pro, 24 gm carb, 0 mg chol,
    4 mg sodium, 0 gm dietary fiber

Appetizers

Herbed Feta Cheese
Basil Cheese Spread
Hot Artichoke Dip
Crab Dip
Texas Crabgrass
Spinach and Artichoke Dip
Shrimp and Basil-Stuffed Mushrooms
Roasted Garlic
Bruschetta with Roasted Garlic and
Parmesan Cheese
Mexican Pizza Appetizer

Herbed Feta Cheese

Cheese connoisseurs will definitely enjoy this creative concoction.

1/2 red bell pepper, cut lengthwise
7 oz. feta cheese, at room temperature
4 oz. fat-free cream cheese, at room temperature
1 1/2 T. herbs de Provence*

*Herbs de Provence may be found in the spice section of your grocery store. Try the Herbs de Provence recipe in this book or use any combination of dried basil, thyme, fennel seed, sage, marjoram and/or rosemary.

1. Remove seeds and stem from red pepper. Place pepper, skin-side up, under broiler until skin turns black. Remove and place in a plastic bag for 10 to 15 minutes. Remove skin and cut into small pieces.
2. Place cheeses and red pepper into a bowl and stir well to combine.
3. Form into a small disk and place on serving plate. Pat herbs onto cheese.
4. Serve with reduced-fat crackers and fresh vegetables.

Yield: 14 servings
Per Serving:
    46 cal, 3 gm fat, 3 gm pro, 1 gm carb, 14 mg chol,
    207 mg sodium, 0 gm dietary fiber

Basil Cheese Spread

A wonderful appetizer when served on fresh French bread.

1 tsp. minced garlic
8 oz. fat-free cream cheese, at room temperature
1/4 c. nonfat sour cream
2 oz. feta cheese, crumbled
1 T. lemon juice
1/4 c. chopped fresh parsley
1/4 c. chopped green onions
1 T. fresh oregano
1 T. chopped fresh basil
1/8 tsp. salt

1. Combine all ingredients using a mixer. (Do not use a blender or food processor.)
2. Refrigerate for a few hours to allow flavors to blend.

Yield: 12 servings
Per Serving:
 37 cal, 1 gm fat, 4 gm pro, 2 gm carb, 8 mg chol,
 196 mg sodium, 0 gm dietary fiber

Hot Artichoke Dip

A hearty-healthy improvement of a favorite dip. We used a little light mayonnaise for the "mayo taste".

1 (14 oz.) can artichoke hearts
1 c. Parmesan cheese
3/4 c. fat-free mayonnaise
1/4 c. light mayonnaise
1/8 tsp. paprika

1. Drain artichokes and cut into small pieces.
2. Mix all ingredients together, except paprika, and place into a small baking dish.
3. Sprinkle mixture with paprika.
4. Bake at 350°F. for 20 to 30 minutes.
5. Serve with fresh vegetables and reduced-fat crackers.

Yield: 11 servings
Per Serving (1/4 cup):
    72 cal, 4 gm fat, 3 gm pro, 6 gm carb, 6 mg chol,
    415 mg sodium, 0 gm dietary fiber

Crab Dip

The light cream cheese makes this low-fat dip seem scrumptiously sinful.

4 oz. light cream cheese
4 oz. fat-free cream cheese
1/2 c. cocktail sauce
5 oz. fresh crab or 1 (6 oz.) can, drained
3 green onions, chopped

1. Combine cheeses and spread into a 9-inch pie dish or similar-size serving dish.
2. Spread cocktail sauce over the top and sprinkle with crab, then green onions.
3. Serve with fresh French bread, fresh vegetables or reduced-fat crackers.

Yield: 8 servings
Per Serving:
   92 cal, 3 gm fat, 8 gm pro, 7 gm carb, 24 mg chol,
   310 mg sodium, 2 gm dietary fiber

Texas Crabgrass

You can also make this ahead of time. Just reheat in the oven at 350 °F. for 15 to 20 minutes until hot.

1 c. chopped onion
Nonstick vegetable cooking spray
1 (10 oz.) pkg. frozen chopped spinach
1/4 c. sherry
5 oz. fresh crab or 1 (6 oz.) can, drained
3/4 c. Parmesan cheese

1. Sauté onion in skillet that has been coated with cooking spray.
2. Defrost spinach and squeeze out all water.
3. Add spinach and sherry to skillet with onion and heat for 2 to 3 minutes.
4. Stir in crab and Parmesan cheese and serve with reduced-fat crackers and fresh vegetables.

Yield: 10 servings
Per Serving:
   57 cal, 2 gm fat, 6 gm pro, 1 gm carb, 16 mg chol,
   234 mg sodium, 1 gm dietary fiber

Spinach and Artichoke Dip

Serve with baked tortilla chips and a mild salsa for double-dipping. Superb!

1 (10 oz.) package frozen chopped spinach
1 (14 oz.) can artichoke hearts, drained & chopped
3/4 c. light sour cream
1 (4 oz.) can chopped green chilies

1. Defrost spinach and squeeze out all water.
2. Stir together all ingredients.
3. Heat in microwave or in oven at 350°F. until hot.

Yield: 8 servings
Per Serving (~1/4 cup):
    46 cal, 2 gm fat, 3 gm pro, 3 gm carb, 8 mg chol,
    208 mg sodium, 2 gm dietary fiber

Shrimp and Basil-Stuffed Mushrooms

8 medium (36 to 40 count) shrimp
1 T. fresh chopped basil or 3/4 tsp. dried basil
1 tsp. minced garlic
1/8 tsp. salt
3/4 tsp. olive oil
1 1/2 T. bread crumbs
2 tsp. Parmesan cheese
12 large mushrooms, stems removed
Nonstick vegetable cooking spray

1. Place shrimp in a pot of boiling water and cook just until water comes back to a boil. Drain water and cool shrimp in refrigerator.
2. Peel and devein shrimp.
3. Cut shrimp into small pieces and combine with all remaining ingredients except mushrooms. Spoon into mushroom caps.
4. Place in baking dish that has been coated with cooking spray.
5. Bake at 375°F. for 15 minutes; serve warm.

Yield: 3 servings
Per Serving (4 mushrooms):
    60 cal, 2 gm fat, 5 gm pro, 5 gm carb, 24 mg chol,
    166 mg sodium, 1 gm dietary fiber

A note about mushrooms: Mushrooms contain a large amount of water. When cooked, they release their water which can make certain recipes soupy. In this recipe, the bread crumbs absorb the excess water and create a fabulous stuffing.

Roasted Garlic

The edges of the garlic will be caramelized; serve on a bread plate, one per person.

6 heads garlic
1 T. olive oil
1 T. chopped fresh basil, thyme or oregano
1/2 tsp. salt
1/4 tsp. pepper

1. Slice top third off each head of garlic.
2. Pour oil in the bottom of a pan just large enough to fit garlic. Stir in herbs, salt and pepper.
3. Place garlic heads, cut-side down, in the pan. Bake at 350°F. for 35 minutes.

Yield: 6 servings
Per Serving (1 head garlic):
   73 cal, 2 gm fat, 2 gm pro, 11 gm carb, 0 mg chol,
   184 mg sodium, 1 gm dietary fiber

Bruschetta with Roasted Garlic and Parmesan Cheese

An Italian treat you don't have to avoid anymore.
Bon Appetit!

Roasted Garlic (see previous recipe)
1 (8 oz.) fresh French baguette
2 oz. (1/2 c.) fresh grated Parmesan cheese

1. Squeeze garlic out of pods and mash to make a paste.
2. Cut bread into 24 slices and spread with garlic paste.
3. Top each piece of bread with 1 teaspoon Parmesan cheese and place under broiler just until bread is toasted and cheese is melted.

Yield: 12 servings
Per Serving (2 slices):
   110 cal, 3 gm fat, 5 gm pro, 15 gm carb, 4 mg chol,
   295 mg sodium, 1 gm dietary fiber

Mexican Pizza Appetizer

A low-fat pleaser, with a spicy kick.

1 c. chopped tomatoes
4 oz. (1 c.) part-skim mozzarella cheese, shredded
1/2 c. chopped cilantro
2 to 3 T. sliced jalapeños
1 (14 oz.) pizza crust*

*We used Kabuli pizza crust which is made without fat and available in the grocery store.

1. Stir tomatoes, cheese, cilantro and jalapeños together.
2. Spread mixture over pizza crust.
3. Bake at 400°F. for 10 minutes. Cut into 16 pieces.

Yield: 16 servings
Per Serving:
    90 cal, 1 gm fat, 4 gm pro, 14 gm carb, 4 mg chol,
    130 mg sodium, 1 gm dietary fiber

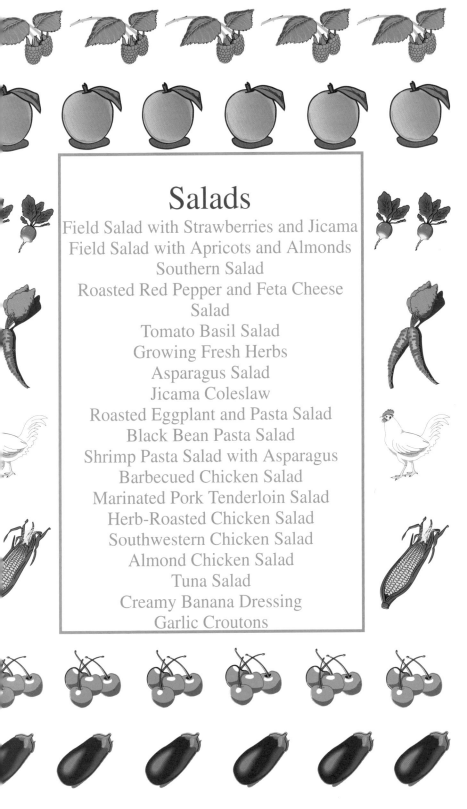

Salads

Field Salad with Strawberries and Jicama
Field Salad with Apricots and Almonds
Southern Salad
Roasted Red Pepper and Feta Cheese
Salad
Tomato Basil Salad
Growing Fresh Herbs
Asparagus Salad
Jicama Coleslaw
Roasted Eggplant and Pasta Salad
Black Bean Pasta Salad
Shrimp Pasta Salad with Asparagus
Barbecued Chicken Salad
Marinated Pork Tenderloin Salad
Herb-Roasted Chicken Salad
Southwestern Chicken Salad
Almond Chicken Salad
Tuna Salad
Creamy Banana Dressing
Garlic Croutons

Field Salad with Strawberries and Jicama

A beautiful salad!

8 c. torn curly lettuce (escarole, endive, red leaf, radicchio,
  Boston)
1/4 c. fresh basil leaves
1/2 c. chopped green onions
1 c. sliced jicama or Granny Smith apple
1 c. sliced strawberries
1/4 c. almond slices, toasted*
Strawberry vinegar or balsamic vinegar (optional)

*To toast nuts, place them under broiler just until lightly browned
and fragrant. This takes just a couple of minutes, so watch them
carefully!

1. Combine all ingredients and toss with strawberry vinegar or
    balsamic vinegar. (If using balsamic vinegar, place on greens
    first and then add jicama or apples so they do not turn brown
    from the vinegar.)

Yield: 6 servings
Per Serving:
  66 cal, 3 gm fat, 3 gm pro, 5 gm carb, 0 mg chol,
  18 mg sodium, 3 gm dietary fiber

Field Salad with Apricots and Almonds

For a main course top with a grilled chicken breast. The apricots add beta-carotene.

8 c. torn red leaf lettuce
1 c. torn radicchio
1/2 c. chopped fresh parsley
1 c. fresh or canned apricots in light syrup, cut into 1/2-inch
    strips
3 T. sliced almonds, toasted*
Balsamic vinegar or reduced-calorie dressing (optional)

*To toast nuts, place under broiler just until lightly browned and fragrant. This takes just a couple of minutes, so watch them carefully!

1.   Combine lettuce, radicchio and parsley.
2.   Divide between 6 salad plates and top with apricots and almonds.
3.   Drizzle with balsamic vinegar or reduced-calorie dressing.

Yield: 6 servings
Per Serving:
    59 cal, 3 gm fat, 3 gm pro, 5 gm carb, 0 mg chol,
    17 mg sodium, 3 gm dietary fiber

Southern Salad

"Ya'll come back now, ya hear!" (They will!)

Croutons:
1 (8 1/2 oz.) box Jiffy corn muffin mix
1/3 c. skim milk
2 egg whites or 1/4 c. egg substitute
Nonstick vegetable cooking spray

1. Combine muffin mix, skim milk, and egg whites or egg substitute; stir just until moistened.
2. Spread batter into a 9x9-inch pan that has been coated with cooking spray.
3. Bake at 350°F. for 15 to 20 minutes until golden brown.
4. Cool for 10 minutes and then cut into 9 pieces. Cut each square into 9 more pieces and place under broiler in oven and toast for just a few minutes.

Pecans:
1/2 T. margarine
18 pecan halves
1/8 tsp. salt
1/2 tsp. sugar

1. Melt margarine in small skillet. Add pecans and cook over low heat for 3 to 4 minutes, stirring constantly.
2. Place in a small baking dish and sprinkle with salt and sugar. Bake at 350°F. for 15 minutes, stirring once or twice.

Salad:
12 c. torn red leaf lettuce
9 T. balsamic vinegar

1. Divide lettuce among 9 plates. Drizzle each with vinegar and top with pecans and croutons.

Yield: 9 servings
Per Serving:
163 cal, 6 gm fat, 4 gm pro, 20 gm carb, 0 mg chol,
358 mg sodium, 3 gm fiber

Roasted Red Pepper and Feta Cheese Salad

I created this salad when I saw a great sale on red peppers that I just couldn't pass up. The feta cheese will melt a little, adding a very rich flavor.

4 red bell peppers
2 oz. feta cheese, crumbled
1/8 tsp. salt
1/8 tsp. pepper
2 tsp. fresh oregano or 1/2 tsp. dried oregano
4 c. torn Romaine lettuce

1. Cut peppers in half lengthwise, removing seeds and stem. Place peppers, skin-side up, under broiler until skins are black. Remove and place in a plastic bag for 10 to 15 minutes. Remove skins and cut into bite-size pieces.
2. Stir cheese, salt, pepper and oregano into peppers while still warm.
3. Place lettuce on plates and spoon pepper mixture over the top.

Yield: 4 servings
Per Serving:
    67 cal, 3 gm fat, 4 gm pro, 4 gm carb, 13 mg chol,
    231 mg sodium, 3 gm dietary fiber

Tomato Basil Salad

3 1/2 c. Roma tomato wedges
2 T. chopped fresh basil
2 oz. feta cheese, crumbled
1 tsp. olive oil
2 tsp. lemon juice
1/8 tsp. salt
Dash of pepper

1. Combine all ingredients and serve.

Yield: 5 servings
Per Serving:
     66 cal, 4 gm fat, 3 gm pro, 6 gm carb, 10 mg chol,
     192 mg sodium, 2 gm dietary fiber

Growing Fresh Herbs...

There is something special about making a trip to the garden to cut fresh herbs for the dish you are preparing. Whether you have a plentiful garden or just a few terra-cotta pots on a balcony, fresh herbs add flavor and a natural feeling to your cooking. Favorites to grow include basil, oregano, mint and rosemary. Grow herbs by planting seeds in the spring or by purchasing a few small plants from your neighborhood nursery. A small container of fresh herbs cost around $1.50 in the grocery store, a small plant costs $1.00 from the nursery. Even if it's only used for one recipe, the venture is still cost effective. Look for opportunities to make use of your gardening and cooking prowess by trying recipes such as the following: Steamed Salmon with Fresh Herbs, Pesto Sauce, Basil Cheese Spread, Roasted Garlic, Tomato Basil Pasta with Pine Nuts and many, many others. When substituting dry herbs, use 1/4 to 1/3 amount of dried herbs for fresh herbs. For example, 1 cup fresh equals 1/4 to 1/3 cup dried.

Asparagus Salad

Buy asparagus in the spring when the prices are low and then enjoy this salad at your favorite picnic spot. A good spot in Dallas is Dallas Blooms at The Dallas Arboretum.

3/4 lb. fresh asparagus
1 tomato, chopped
1 T. capers
2 tsp. Dijon mustard
4 green onions, chopped
Dash of pepper
2 tsp. olive oil
1 T. white wine vinegar

1. Break off bottom 1/4 of asparagus and blanch in boiling water for 2 minutes. Drain and run cold water over asparagus.
2. Cut asparagus into thirds and combine with remaining ingredients.

Yield: 4 servings
Per Serving:
    42 cal, 3 gm fat, 2 gm pro, 4 gm carb, 0 mg chol,
    43 mg sodium, 2 gm dietary fiber

Jicama Coleslaw

Discover jicama in this all-time favorite salad.

3 T. light mayonnaise
3 T. light sour cream
1 T. sugar
1/4 tsp. pepper
2 1/2 c. shredded cabbage
1/2 c. grated carrots
1/2 c. chopped cilantro
1/2 c. chopped green pepper
1 c. chopped jicama

1. Stir mayonnaise, sour cream, sugar and pepper together.
2. Combine all vegetables and stir in dressing.

Yield: 6 servings
Per Serving:
    72 cal, 3 gm fat, 2 gm pro, 8 gm carb, 5 mg chol,
    78 mg sodium, 2 gm dietary fiber

Roasted Eggplant and Pasta Salad

The hardiness of eggplant and pasta allow you to be extravagant with seasonings.

1 (1 lb.) eggplant
1 3/4 tsp. salt, divided use
Nonstick vegetable cooking spray
8 oz. dried penne pasta
1 1/2 T. olive oil
3 T. chopped fresh basil
3 T. chopped Italian parsley
2 T. red wine vinegar
1 tsp. minced garlic
1/8 tsp. pepper
1 tsp. oregano
1 c. chopped tomatoes

1. Slice eggplant into 1/2-inch-thick slices. Sprinkle both sides of eggplant with 1 teaspoon salt and place in a colander in sink. Let sit for 30 minutes.
2. Rinse eggplant well.
3. Spray both sides of eggplant slices with cooking spray and lay in a large baking dish in 1 layer. Bake at 450°F. for 15 minutes, turning once. Remove from oven and cut into bite-size pieces.
4. Cook pasta according to package directions, omitting salt and fat.
5. Combine oil, basil, parsley, vinegar, garlic, 3/4 teaspoon salt, pepper and oregano.
6. Combine pasta, eggplant and tomatoes; stir in dressing.

Yield: 10 servings
Per Serving:
    120 cal, 3 gm fat, 4 gm pro, 19 gm carb, 0 mg chol,
    166 mg sodium, 2 gm dietary fiber

Black Bean Pasta Salad

Yellow corn and green onions add color for the eye and appeals to the palate.

6 oz. dried orzo pasta
2 oz. (1/2 c.) reduced-fat Monterey Jack cheese, shredded
1 c. cooked or canned black beans, drained & rinsed of any bean
   liquid
1/4 c. chopped green onions
1 c. frozen corn, defrosted
1/2 c. chopped cilantro
1/2 c. fat-free salad dressing (ranch, lime-cilantro, etc.)

1. Cook pasta according to package directions, omitting salt and
    fat; drain and allow to cool.
2. Stir in remaining ingredients.

Yield: 10 servings
Per Serving (1/2 cup):
    126 cal, 2 gm fat, 6 gm pro, 22 gm carb, 3 mg chol,
    203 mg sodium, 3 gm dietary fiber

Shrimp Pasta Salad with Asparagus

Easy and elegant for a luncheon menu.

1 lb. dried bow tie (farfalle) pasta
1 lb. fresh asparagus
1 lb. (36 to 40 count) shrimp
2/3 c. reduced-calorie Italian dressing
2 tsp. Dijon mustard
1/4 c. chopped green onions
2 tomatoes, chopped
2 tsp. basil
2 tsp. oregano
3 oz. (3/4 c.) fresh grated Parmesan cheese

1. Cook pasta according to package directions, omitting salt and fat; drain and allow to cool.
2. Break off bottom 1/4 of asparagus. Steam for 4 to 6 minutes until asparagus is tender-crisp and bright green. Cooking time will depend on thickness of asparagus.
3. Place shrimp in a pot of boiling water and cook just until water comes back to a boil; drain. Place in refrigerator to cool.
4. Peel and devein shrimp.
5. Stir together Italian dressing and mustard.
6. Stir together pasta, asparagus, shrimp, dressing and remaining ingredients.

Yield: 12 servings
Per Serving:
    208 cal, 4 gm fat, 13 gm pro, 30 gm carb, 34 mg chol,
    289 mg sodium, 2 gm dietary fiber

Barbecued Chicken Salad

This whole-meal salad is a colorful way to use up leftover barbecued chicken.

2 (4 oz.) boneless, skinless chicken breasts
2 T. barbecue sauce
4 c. torn red leaf lettuce
1/2 c. frozen corn, defrosted
1 c. chopped jicama
1/2 c. cooked or canned black beans, rinsed & drained of any
    bean liquid
1/2 c. chopped cilantro
1/2 Anaheim pepper or green bell pepper, chopped
2 T. lime juice
1/8 tsp. salt
1/3 c. (5 1/3 T.) reduced-fat Monterey Jack cheese, shredded
4 baked tortilla chips, broken into small pieces
4 T. fat-free ranch dressing (optional)

1. Place chicken breasts in a small pan. Spread barbecue sauce
    evenly over chicken. Bake at 350°F. for 30 minutes or until no
    longer pink inside. Remove from pan, and when cool, cut into
    small pieces.
2. Toss lettuce, corn, jicama, black beans, cilantro and pepper
    with lime juice and salt. Divide between 2 plates.
3. Top with chicken, cheese and chips. Drizzle with ranch dress-
    ing, if desired.

Yield: 2 servings
Per Serving:
    386 cal, 7 gm fat, 41 gm pro, 41 gm carb, 85 mg chol,
    621 mg sodium, 6 gm dietary fiber

Marinated Pork Tenderloin Salad

This salad uses a favorite recipe from our first cookbook.

12 c. torn lettuce (red leaf, radicchio, escarole, and/or Boston)
1 1/2 red bell peppers, cut into strips
4 green onions, chopped
1 1/2 c. sliced mushrooms
Marinated Pork Tenderloin (see Index)
3 T. sliced almonds
Balsamic vinegar or fat-free dressing (optional)

1. In a large bowl, combine salad greens, red pepper, onions and mushrooms; toss gently.
2. Divide mixture among 8 plates.
3. Thinly slice meat and arrange on salads.
4. Sprinkle with almonds and serve with balsamic vinegar or fat-free dressing.

Yield: 8 servings
Per Serving:
    237 cal, 9 gm fat, 30 gm pro, 7 gm carb, 80 mg chol,
    186 mg sodium, 4 gm dietary fiber

Herb-Roasted Chicken Salad

For a low-fat meal, serve with a fruit salad and wholewheat roll.

1 Herb-Roasted Chicken (see Index)
1/4 c. light sour cream
1/4 c. fat-free mayonnaise
1/4 tsp. salt
1 1/2 c. chopped red apple
1/2 c. chopped celery
3 T. chopped toasted walnuts*
1 T. fresh rosemary or 1 tsp. dried rosemary

*To toast nuts, place under broiler just until lightly browned and fragrant. This takes just a couple of minutes, so watch them carefully!

1. Brush seasoning on chicken skin into a bowl.
2. Remove chicken from bone and shred into small pieces, discarding skin and fat.
3. Stir sour cream, mayonnaise and salt together.
4. Add chicken, apple, celery, walnuts and rosemary to bowl with seasonings.
5. Stir in dressing.
6. If chicken was warm when taken from bone, refrigerate salad for 2 hours.

Yield: 6 servings
Per Serving:
222 cal, 9 gm fat, 25 gm pro, 9 gm carb, 72 mg chol, 305 mg sodium, 1 gm dietary fiber

Southwestern Chicken Salad

An almost guilt-free chicken salad you can serve often.

2 (4 oz.) boneless, skinless chicken breasts, grilled and thinly
    sliced
1/4 c. chopped cilantro
1 1/2 T. fat-free mayonnaise
1 1/2 T. light sour cream
Dash of ground cumin
Dash of pepper
1 T. pine nuts, toasted*

*To toast nuts, place under broiler just until lightly browned and
fragrant. This takes just a couple of minutes, so watch them carefully!

1. Combine all ingredients and serve.

Yield: 2 servings
Per Serving:
    197 cal, 7 gm fat, 29 gm pro, 5 gm carb, 76 mg chol,
    217 mg sodium, 1 gm dietary fiber

Almond Chicken Salad

4 (4 oz.) boneless, skinless chicken breasts
1 1/2 c. low-sodium chicken broth
1/4 c. toasted almonds*
1/2 c. chopped celery
2 hard-boiled egg whites, chopped
2 T. light mayonnaise
2 T. fat-free mayonnaise
1 tsp. lemon juice
1/4 tsp. hot pepper sauce
2 T. pickle relish
1/8 tsp. salt
1/2 tsp. pepper
5 lettuce leaves (optional)
Paprika, to taste

*To toast nuts, place under broiler just until lightly browned and fragrant. This takes just a couple of minutes, so watch them carefully!

1. Place chicken breasts in a 9x9-inch pan and pour chicken broth over them.
2. Cover the pan with a sheet of aluminum foil and bake at 350°F. for 30 minutes. Allow chicken to cool in liquid.
3. Shred chicken into bite-size pieces. Put in a bowl with almonds, celery and egg whites.
4. Stir together mayonnaise, lemon juice, pepper sauce, pickle relish, salt and pepper. Fold dressing into chicken mixture and chill.
5. Serve on a lettuce leaf and sprinkle with paprika.

Yield: 5 servings
Per Serving:
    197 cal, 8 gm fat, 24 gm pro, 5 gm carb, 60 mg chol,
    308 mg sodium, 1 gm dietary fiber

Tuna Salad

Skip the chopped onions, the dill weed adds the necessary pizzazz for this tuna salad.

1 (6 oz.) can tuna in water, drained
1 1/2 T. light mayonnaise
1 1/2 T. light sour cream
1 tsp. dill weed
1/8 tsp. pepper

1. Combine all ingredients and serve between 2 slices of bread or just by itself.

Yield: 2 servings
Per Serving:
   170 cal, 7 gm fat, 24 gm pro, 4 gm carb, 36 mg chol,
   383 mg sodium, 9 gm dietary fiber

Creamy Banana Dressing

A unique way to use up an overripe banana and awaken any fruit salad.

1/2 c. low-fat cottage cheese (1% or 2% fat)
1 banana
2 T. fruit juice
1 T. honey

1. In a food processor or blender, combine all ingredients and process until smooth.

Yield: 7 servings
Per Serving (2 tablespoons):
   38 cal, <1 gm fat, 2 gm pro, 7 gm carb, 1 mg chol,
   66 mg sodium, 0 gm dietary fiber

Garlic Croutons

Homemade breads made without preservatives tend to go stale quickly. Croutons are an ideal alternative to stale bread.

3 slices bread
Nonstick vegetable cooking spray
Garlic powder, to taste
Pepper, to taste

1. Cut bread into 1/2-inch pieces. Place on baking pan in a single layer. Coat bread with cooking spray and sprinkle with garlic powder and pepper.
2. Toast, using broil setting on oven, until slightly browned. This also works well using a toaster oven; place in oven and hit toast button.
3. Allow to cool and transfer to an airtight jar.

Yield: 8 servings
Per Serving (1/4 cup):
    28 cal, <1 gm fat, 1 gm pro, 5 gm carb, 0 mg chol,
    51 mg sodium, 0 gm dietary fiber

Vegetables

Asparagus with Parmesan Cheese
Sautéed Broccoli and Sugar Snap Peas
Brussels Sprouts with Shallots
Orange-Glazed Carrots
Raspberry Carrots
Carrots, Zucchini and Tomatoes in
Cheese Sauce
Corn Casserole
Corn and Tomatoes with Curry
Green Beans with Blue Cheese
Lemon Thyme Green Beans
Okra and Tomatoes
Roasted Peppers with Shallots
Sautéed Spinach with Balsamic Vinegar
Baked Acorn Squash
Summer Squash Casserole

Red Peppered Yellow Squash

Zucchini with Oregano and Mozzarella Cheese

Carole's Roasted Vegetables

Penny's Roasted Vegetables

Roasted Potatoes and Green Beans

Pesto-Crusted Potato Wedges

Blue Cheese Scalloped Potatoes

Sweet Potato Casserole

Fried Potatoes

Rice and Bulgar Timbales

Refried Black Beans

Asparagus with Parmesan Cheese

Simple and Delicious!

1 lb. fresh asparagus
2 T. fresh grated Parmesan cheese
1 tsp. fresh lemon juice
Pepper, to taste

1. Break off bottom 1/4 of asparagus. Steam for 4 to 6 minutes until asparagus is tender-crisp and bright green. Cooking time will depend on the thickness of the asparagus.
2. Divide evenly among 4 plates and sprinkle each with 1/2 tablespoon cheese, 1/4 teaspoon lemon juice, and pepper. If cheese does not melt sufficiently, briefly microwave each plate.

Yield: 4 servings
Per Serving:
   30 cal, 1 gm fat, 3 gm pro, 3 gm carb, 3 mg chol,
   69 mg sodium, 2 gm dietary fiber

Sautéed Broccoli and Sugar Snap Peas

Because the processing of vegetables from the garden to frozen is so quick, frozen veggies can be as nutritious as fresh ones.

1 lb. frozen broccoli
1 lb. frozen sugar snap peas
1 T. olive oil
2 tsp. minced garlic
8 oz. sliced mushrooms
1/2 tsp. salt
1/4 tsp. pepper

1. Microwave broccoli and sugar snap peas according to package directions; drain.
2. Heat oil in a large skillet. Add garlic and mushrooms; sauté for 6 to 8 minutes.
3. Add broccoli, sugar snap peas, salt and pepper; cook until hot.

Yield: 9 servings
Per Serving (3/4 cup):
   55 cal, 2 gm fat, 4 gm pro, 4 gm carb, 0 mg chol,
   250 mg sodium, 3 gm dietary fiber

Brussels Sprouts with Shallots

A great introductory dish for any Brussels sprouts doubter.

4 c. fresh Brussels sprouts
1/3 c. water
1 tsp. olive oil
1/2 c. chopped shallots
3 oz. Canadian bacon, chopped

1. Remove discolored outer leaves from Brussels sprouts and trim ends.
2. Place Brussels sprouts and water in covered dish and microwave for 4 minutes; drain.
3. Heat olive oil in skillet. Add shallots and sauté for 5 minutes.
4. Add Canadian bacon and Brussels sprouts and cook for 2 to 3 minutes, stirring so Brussels sprouts do not stick.

Yield: 6 servings
Per Serving:
  82 cal, 2 gm fat, 6 gm pro, 11 gm carb, 8 mg chol,
  243 mg sodium, 4 gm dietary fiber

Orange-Glazed Carrots

Look familiar? There is no butter in this recipe...that means no fat in these glazed carrots.

2 lb. carrots, peeled & sliced
1/4 c. water
2 T. brown sugar
2 T. sugar
3 T. orange juice
1 tsp. cinnamon
1/2 tsp. allspice
1 tsp. vanilla extract

1. Place carrots and water in a covered dish and microwave for 5 to 7 minutes, just until tender.
2. Drain water and add remaining ingredients; stir.
3. Bake at 350°F. for 15 to 20 minutes.

Yield: 8 servings
Per Serving:
   81 cal, 0 gm fat, 1 gm pro, 19 gm carb, 0 mg chol,
   77 mg sodium, 4 gm dietary fiber

Raspberry Carrots

The hint of raspberry gives this vegetable dish a new twist. Serve with Garlic-Roasted Pork Loin.

6 carrots, thinly sliced
1/4 c. water
1 1/2 tsp. margarine
Dash of salt
2 to 4 tsp. raspberry vinegar
2 tsp. brown sugar
Chopped parsley (optional)

1. Place carrots and water in a covered dish and microwave for 5 to 7 minutes, just until tender.
2. Drain water from carrots.
3. Add margarine, salt, raspberry vinegar and sugar; stir to combine.
4. Microwave for 1 to 2 more minutes.
5. Garnish with parsley, if desired.

Yield: 3 servings
Per Serving:
   77 cal, 2 gm fat, 1 gm pro, 11 gm carb, 0 mg chol,
   107 mg sodium, 3 gm dietary fiber

Carrots, Zucchini and Tomatoes in Cheese Sauce

This low-fat hearty vegetable dish will satisfy the most discriminating palates and is a good source of beta-carotene, vitamin C and fiber. Serve with Beef in Shallot Sauce and baked potatoes.

3 c. sliced carrots, or peeled mini carrots
1/4 c. water
3 c. sliced zucchini
3 tomatoes, chopped
Nonstick vegetable cooking spray
2 T. cornstarch
1 1/2 c. skim milk
1 c. (4 oz.) reduced-fat Cheddar cheese, shredded
1/4 tsp. salt
Dash of cayenne pepper

1. Place carrots and water in a covered dish and microwave for 5 to 7 minutes, just until tender.
2. Layer zucchini, carrots and tomatoes in a 9x13-inch baking dish that has been coated with cooking spray.
3. In a saucepan, stir cornstarch into milk. Add 1/2 cup cheese, salt and cayenne pepper; cook until smooth and thickened.
4. Pour sauce over vegetables and top with remaining cheese.
5. Bake at 375°F. for 30 minutes.

Yield: 8 servings
Per Serving:
    114 cal, 3 gm fat, 7 gm pro, 13 gm carb, 8 mg chol,
    199 mg sodium, 4 gm dietary fiber

Corn Casserole

2 (16 1/2 oz.) cans cream-style corn
1/4 c. chopped green pepper
1/4 c. chopped onion
1 T. chopped pimento
1 c. egg substitute
1 T. flour
1/8 tsp. pepper
Nonstick vegetable cooking spray

1. Place all ingredients in a large bowl and stir to combine.
2. Pour into a 9x9-inch baking dish that has been coated with cooking spray and bake at 325°F. for 1 hour.

Yield: 6 servings
Per Serving:
    138 cal, 1 gm fat, 6 gm pro, 31 gm carb, 0 mg chol,
    498 mg sodium, 2 gm dietary fiber

Corn and Tomatoes with Curry

Serve with lightly-seasoned grilled meats.

2 tsp. margarine
3/4 c. chopped onion
2 (10 oz.) package frozen corn
1 1/2 c. chopped tomatoes
1/4 tsp. salt
1 tsp. curry powder

1. Heat margarine in a large skillet and sauté onion until transparent.
2. Stir in remaining ingredients and cook for 5 minutes.

Yield: 9 servings
Per Serving:
    73 cal, 2 gm fat, 2 gm pro, 13 gm carb, 0 mg chol,
    123 mg sodium, 2 gm dietary fiber

Green Beans with Blue Cheese

Easy and always a favorite!

3/4 lb. (3 c.) fresh green beans
1/4 c. water
3/4 oz. blue cheese

1. Trim ends of green beans and cut in half.
2. Place green beans and water in a covered dish and microwave for 6 minutes.
3. Drain water and crumble blue cheese over top. Cover and allow cheese to melt.

Yield: 4 servings
Per Serving:
    52 cal, 2 gm fat, 3 gm pro, 7 gm carb, 4 mg chol,
    78 mg sodium, 2 gm dietary fiber

Lemon Thyme Green Beans

1 lb. (4 c.) fresh green beans
1/4 c. water
1 T. lemon juice
2 tsp. thyme

1. Trim ends of green beans and cut in half.
2. Place green beans and water in a covered dish and microwave for 6 minutes.
3. Drain water from green beans.
4. Add lemon juice and thyme; stir to combine.

Yield: 4 servings
Per Serving:
    43 cal, 0 gm fat, 2 gm pro, 9 gm carb, 0 mg chol,
    4 mg sodium, 2 gm dietary fiber

Okra and Tomatoes

We used liquid smoke to replace the flavor that this dish has when made with bacon drippings.

1 lb. fresh okra
2 tsp. olive oil
1 onion, chopped
2 tomatoes, chopped
1 tsp. liquid smoke
1/4 tsp. salt
1/4 tsp. pepper
1/8 tsp. cayenne pepper
1/2 tsp. sugar

1. Remove tops of okra and slice pods crosswise in 1/4-inch pieces.
2. Heat oil in a large skillet. Sauté okra for 10 minutes, stirring frequently.
3. Stir in onions and sauté until onions are transparent.
4. Add remaining ingredients; cook over low heat for 2 to 3 minutes.

Yield: 5 servings
Per Serving:
    62 cal, 2 gm fat, 2 gm pro, 11 gm carb, 0 mg chol,
    117 mg sodium, 4 gm dietary fiber

Roasted Peppers with Shallots

Great Presentation!

1 3/4 tsp. olive oil, divided use
3/4 c. whole peeled shallots, cut in half
1 c. cherry tomatoes, cut in half
1 T. fresh or 3/4 tsp. dried oregano
1 tsp. sugar
1/8 tsp. salt
1/8 tsp. pepper
2 red bell peppers, cut in half lengthwise & seeds removed

1. In a small skillet, beat 1 teaspoon olive oil and sauté shallots for 5 minutes.
2. Transfer shallots to a bowl and add tomatoes, oregano, sugar, salt and pepper; toss gently.
3. Place red peppers in a baking dish and brush with remaining 3/4 teaspoon olive oil.
4. Fill peppers with shallot mixture.
5. Bake at 400°F. for 35 minutes.

Yield: 4 servings
Per Serving:
    64 cal, 2 gm fat, 2 gm pro, 9 gm carb, 0 mg chol,
    75 mg sodium, 1 gm dietary fiber

Sautéed Spinach with Balsamic Vinegar

Spinach is a great source of the antioxidants, beta-carotene and vitamin C. Low in calories, it is also a good source of dietary fiber.

1 tsp. olive oil
5 c. fresh spinach with stems removed
1/2 T. balsamic vinegar
Dash of salt & pepper

1. Heat olive oil in a saucepan. Add spinach and sauté until just wilted.
2. Sprinkle with vinegar, salt and pepper.

Yield: 2 servings
Per Serving:
    55 cal, 3 gm fat, 4 gm pro, 5 gm carb, 0 mg chol,
    174 mg sodium, 4 gm dietary fiber

A Squash for all Seasons

Baked Acorn Squash

1 apple, chopped
1/2 c. raisins
2 tsp. margarine
3 T. brown sugar, firmly packed
1 T. orange juice
1 T. reduce-calorie maple syrup
1 tsp. cinnamon
1/4 tsp. ground cloves
2 acorn squash

1. Mix apple and raisins together.
2. In a small saucepan, melt margarine. Add sugar and stir until it dissolves. Add orange juice, syrup, cinnamon and cloves. Pour over apple mixture and mix well.
3. Slice squash lengthwise and scoop out seeds and strings. Puncture cavity several times with a fork, being careful not to pierce skin.
4. Fill squares with apple mixture and cover with foil.
5. Place in a baking dish and bake at 400°F. for 1 hour.

Yield: 4 servings
Per Serving (1/2 squash):
   180 cal, 3 gm fat, 2 gm pro, 41 mg carb, 0 mg chol,
   40 mg sodium, 5 gm dietary fiber

Summer Squash Casserole

3 lb. yellow squash, thinly sliced
1/2 c. water
3/4 c. egg substitute
2 T. cornstarch
1 c. evaporated skim milk
1/2 tsp. salt
3/4 tsp. pepper
3/4 c. chopped onion
3 T. sugar
Nonstick vegetable cooking spray
1 oz. (1/4 c.) reduced-fat Cheddar cheese, shredded

1.   Place squash and water in a large covered dish. Microwave 8 to 10 minutes until squash is tender; drain well. Slightly mash squash.
2.   In a large bowl, combine squash with remaining ingredients except cheese. Pour into a 9x13-inch baking dish that has been coated with cooking spray.
3.   Top mixture with cheese.
4.   Bake at 350°F. for 45 minutes or until set.

Yield: 10 servings
Per Serving:
    87 cal, 1 gm fat, 6 gm pro, 17 gm carb, 3 mg chol,
    177 mg sodium, 2 gm dietary fiber

Red Peppered Yellow Squash

A very colorful dish that appeals to both the eye and the palate.

2 lb. yellow squash, sliced
1/4 c. water
2 tsp. olive oil
1/3 c. chopped red bell pepper
1 T. chopped fresh basil

1. Place sliced squash and water in a covered dish and microwave for 5 minutes.
2. While squash is cooking, sauté red pepper in olive oil for 2 to 3 minutes, adding basil during last minute of cooking.
3. Drain squash and combine with red pepper and basil.

Yield: 8 servings
Per Serving:
    34 cal, 1 gm fat, 1 gm pro, 6 gm carb, 0 mg chol,
    2 mg sodium, 2 gm dietary fiber

Zucchini with Oregano and Mozzarella Cheese

Never underestimate the palate-pleasing power of lemon juice. Lemon juice adds flavor and flamboyance to any vegetable dish.

4 c. thinly-sliced zucchini
1/2 c. water
4 tsp. fresh or 1 tsp. dried oregano
1 T. lemon juice
1 1/2 oz. (6 T.) part-skim mozzarella cheese, shredded

1. Place zucchini and water in a covered dish. Cook for 5 to 7 minutes until tender.
2. Drain water and stir in oregano and lemon juice.
3. Top with cheese and microwave for another 1 to 2 minutes to melt cheese.

Yield: 5 servings
Per Serving:
    49 cal, 2 gm fat, 3 gm pro, 6 gm carb, 5 mg chol,
    49 mg sodium, 1 gm dietary fiber

Carole's Roasted Vegetables

A tasty way to enjoy your "5 a day". *

8 yellow squash, sliced
6 zucchini, sliced
3 red onions, cut into wedges
1 red bell pepper, cut into strips
1 poblano pepper, cut into strips
Nonstick vegetable cooking spray
1 1/2 T. olive oil
1 T. minced garlic
3/4 tsp. salt
3/4 tsp. pepper
8 oz. whole mushrooms

1. Place squash, zucchini, onion and peppers in an oversized (larger than 9x13-inch) baking dish, or 2 smaller ones, that have been coated with cooking spray.
2. In a small bowl, stir together oil, garlic, salt and pepper. Pour over vegetable mixture and stir to coat all vegetables.
3. Bake, covered, at 400°F. for 15 minutes, stirring twice.
4. Remove vegetables from oven and add mushrooms. Stir to coat vegetables.
5. Bake an additional 10 minutes.

Yield: 12 servings
Per Serving:
    58 cal, 2 gm fat, 3 gm pro, 7 gm carb, 0 mg chol,
    287 mg sodium, 2 gm dietary fiber

*The National Cancer Institute recommends that we con-
sume a variety of fruits and vegetables. Strive for a mini-
mum of 5 servings per day.*

Penny's Roasted Vegetables

Simply, the very best way to eat your veggies!

2 lb. small new potatoes, quartered
1 c. sliced carrots
1 red onion, cut into wedges
Nonstick vegetable cooking spray
1 1/2 T. olive oil
3 garlic cloves, minced
3 T. fresh lemon juice
1 tsp. rosemary, crushed
1 tsp. oregano, crushed
1 tsp. salt, divided use
1/2 tsp. pepper
3/4 tsp. lemon pepper
1/2 small eggplant, cut into 1-inch pieces
8 oz. whole mushrooms
1 red bell pepper, cut into 1/2-inch strips
1 yellow bell pepper, cut into 1/2-inch strips
1 green bell pepper, cut into 1/2-inch strips

1. Place potatoes, carrots and onions in a 9x13-inch baking dish that has been coated with cooking spray.
2. In a small bowl, stir together oil, garlic, lemon juice, rosemary, oregano, 3/4 teaspoon salt, pepper and lemon pepper. Pour over potato mixture and stir to coat all vegetables.
3. Bake at 450°F. for 30 minutes, stirring twice.
4. Place eggplant pieces in a strainer and sprinkle with 1/4 teaspoon salt. Allow to stand for 30 minutes and then rinse well.
5. Remove vegetables from oven and add eggplant, mushrooms and peppers. Stir to coat vegetables.
6. Bake an additional 15 minutes.

Yield: 10 servings
Per Serving:
155 cal, 3 gm fat, 4 gm pro, 27 gm carb, 0 mg chol,
203 mg sodium, 4 gm dietary fiber

Roasted Potatoes
and Green Beans

1 3/4 lb. green beans, trimmed & cut in half
1 3/4 lb. new potatoes, cut into bite-size pieces
Nonstick vegetable cooking spray
1 T. olive oil
1 T. minced garlic
1/4 tsp. salt
1/4 tsp. pepper
2 T. fresh thyme or 2 tsp. dried thyme

1. Place green beans and potatoes in a 9x13-inch pan that has been coated with cooking spray.
2. Stir together oil, garlic, salt, pepper and thyme. Pour over vegetables and stir to coat.
3. Bake at 350°F. for 1 hour, stirring every 15 minutes.

Yield: 8 servings
Per Serving:
    128 cal, 2 gm fat, 4 gm pro, 21 gm carb, 0 mg chol,
    79 mg sodium, 5 gm dietary fiber

Pesto-Crusted Potato Wedges

Serve as an alternative to French fries or as an appealing appetizer.

4 (4-inch) baking potatoes
1/4 c. Pesto Sauce (see Index)

1. Prick potatoes a few times with a fork and bake at 400°F. for 1 hour or until tender.
2. Cut each potato in half lengthwise and then in half again to make 4 wedges. Spread cut edges of potato wedges with Pesto Sauce.
3. Place on a baking sheet, pesto-side up. Broil for 4 to 5 minutes or until bubbling.

Yield: 4 servings
Per Serving:
   173 cal, 3 gm fat, 6 gm pro, 29 gm carb, 2 mg chol,
   133 mg sodium, 3 gm dietary fiber

Blue Cheese Scalloped Potatoes

A little blue cheese makes this a wonderful dish. This is a great accompaniment to grilled meats.

2 tsp. olive oil
2 T. minced garlic
2 T. finely-chopped shallots
3 oz. blue cheese
2 1/2 lb. potatoes with skin, thinly sliced
1/8 tsp. white pepper
1 (12 oz.) can evaporated skim milk
3/4 c. skim milk
2/3 c. Parmesan cheese
Nonstick vegetable cooking spray
1 T. parsley

1. In a large pan, heat oil and add garlic and shallots, sautéing for 5 minutes.
2. Add blue cheese and melt over low heat.
3. Add the potatoes and white pepper.
4. Add the evaporated milk and skim milk; bring to a boil, stirring for 2 minutes. Add 7 tablespoons Parmesan cheese and remove from heat.
5. Pour into a large sheet pan that has been coated with cooking spray. Sprinkle with remaining Parmesan cheese and parsley. Bake at 350°F. for 30 minutes, or until golden brown.

Yield: 12 servings
Per Serving:
    205 cal, 5 gm fat, 10 gm pro, 30 gm carb, 12 mg chol,
    286 mg sodium, 4 gm dietary fiber

Sweet Potato Casserole

This great source of beta-carotene replaces the traditional fat-laden Thanksgiving treats.

2 1/2 lb. sweet potatoes, peeled
3/4 c. egg substitute or 6 egg whites
1/2 c. skim milk
3/4 c. brown sugar, firmly packed, divided use
3/4 tsp. salt
Nonstick vegetable cooking spray
1 T. margarine, softened
1/4 c. flour
1/4 c. chopped pecans

1. Cut potatoes into 4 pieces each, and boil for 30 minutes or until tender.
2. Mash potatoes and combine with egg substitute or egg whites, skim milk, 1/4 cup brown sugar and salt; stir well.
3. Pour potato mixture into a 9x13-inch baking dish that has been coated with cooking spray.
4. Stir 1/2 cup brown sugar, margarine, flour and pecans together. Sprinkle over potatoes.
5. Bake at 350°F. for 30 minutes.

Yield: 12 servings
Per Serving:
194 cal, 3 gm fat, 3 gm pro, 37 gm carb, 0 mg chol,
189 mg sodium, 3 gm dietary fiber

Fried Potatoes

Just like Grandmother used to make.

Nonstick vegetable cooking spray
2 tsp. olive oil
2 lb. potatoes, peeled & thinly sliced
1/2 onion, chopped
1/4 to 1/2 c. water
1/2 tsp. salt
1/2 tsp. pepper

1. In a skillet that has been coated with cooking spray, heat oil.
2. Add potatoes and onions. Cover and cook until tender, adding water and stirring occasionally to prevent sticking.
3. Season with salt and pepper; serve.

Yield: 7 servings
Per Serving (3/4 cup):
    91 cal, 1 gm fat, 2 gm pro, 16 gm carb, 0 mg chol,
    201 mg sodium, 2 gm dietary fiber

Rice and Bulgar Timbales

These can be frozen after baking for enjoyment at a moment's notice.

1 c. dried bulgar wheat
2 c. low-sodium chicken broth, defatted*
1 c. cooked rice
1/4 c. chopped green onions
3 T. sliced almonds**
1 T. chopped fresh parsley
4 egg whites or 1/2 c. egg substitute
1/4 c. skim milk
3 T. Pesto Sauce (see Index)
1/2 tsp. salt
1/4 tsp. pepper
Nonstick vegetable cooking spray

*If using canned or homemade broth, defat by placing in refrigerator. When cold, skim fat off top.
**To toast nuts, place under broiler just until lightly browned and fragrant. This takes just a couple of minutes, so watch them carefully!

1. In a small saucepan, combine bulgar and chicken broth. Bring to a boil and simmer, covered, for 15 minutes until bulgar has absorbed the broth.
2. Combine bulgar with remaining ingredients, except cooking spray, stirring well.
3. Spoon mixture into timbale or custard cups that have been coated with cooking spray.
4. Place cups in a baking pan and fill the pan with water so that it comes 1/3 the way up the sides of the cups.
5. Bake at 375°F. for 45 minutes.
6. Remove the pan from the oven and remove cups. Allow to cool for a few minutes and then turn timbales out of cups.

Yield: 8 servings
Per Serving (1 timbale):
143 cal, 3 gm fat, 6 gm pro, 19 gm carb, 1 mg chol,
234 mg sodium, 4 gm dietary fiber

Refried Black Beans

Add chopped green chilies for Southwestern flair.

2 c. cooked or canned black beans, drained, reserving 2 T. bean
     liquid
1/2 tsp. minced garlic
1/8 tsp. cayenne pepper
1/4 tsp. salt
Nonstick vegetable cooking spray

1.   Place all ingredients in food processor or blender, and puree.
2.   Pour into a hot skillet that has been coated with cooking spray,
     and cook until hot.

Yield: 4 servings
Per Serving:
     114 cal, <1 gm fat, 8 gm pro, 13 gm carb, 0 mg chol,
     134 mg sodium, 8 gm dietary fiber

Soups and Chilis

Chicken Poblano Soup

Turkey Vegetable Soup

Canadian Bacon Pizza Soup

Homemade Chicken Broth

Black Bean Chili

Sagamity

Chicken Posole

Chicken Poblano Soup

Never underestimate the warmth that soup brings to the home of the one who serves it. This soup will warm up your taste buds as well.

1 tsp. margarine
1 poblano pepper, chopped
3/4 c. chopped onion
3 garlic cloves, minced
12 oz. evaporated skim milk
1 (17 oz.) can cream-style corn
1 (17 oz.) can corn, drained
1 c. chicken broth*
1/2 c. water
1 1/2 tsp. ground cumin
1/4 c. chopped cilantro, divided use
4 (4 oz.) boneless, skinless chicken breasts, grilled & thinly sliced
1 1/2 oz. (6 T.) reduced-fat Cheddar cheese, shredded

*If using homemade or canned broth, place in refrigerator. When cold, skim fat off the top. To lower sodium further, use low-sodium chicken broth.

1. In a large saucepan, heat margarine and sauté poblano pepper, onion and garlic for 5 minutes.
2. Add evaporated milk, corn, chicken broth, water, cumin and 2 tablespoons cilantro; cook over low heat for 15 minutes.
3. Stir in remaining cilantro and chicken.
4. Ladle into bowls and top each with 1 tablespoon cheese.

Yield: 6 servings
Per Serving:
    282 cal, 5 gm fat, 28 gm pro, 34 gm carb, 54 mg chol,
    760 mg sodium, 2 gm dietary fiber

Turkey Vegetable Soup

A fabulous alternative to leftover Thanksgiving turkey sandwiches.

Nonstick vegetable cooking spray
3/4 c. chopped celery
2 c. sliced carrots
1 large onion, chopped
1 c. sliced mushrooms
5 c. chicken broth, defatted*
2 c. chopped cooked turkey without skin
1 (17 oz.) can cream-style corn
1/2 c. chopped fresh parsley
1/4 tsp. salt
1 tsp. hot pepper sauce
1 1/2 c. dried penne pasta

*If using canned or homemade chicken broth, place in refrigerator. When cold, skim fat off the top.

1. Coat a large saucepan with cooking spray. Add celery, carrots, onions and mushrooms; cook until onions become transparent, stirring occasionally.
2. Add chicken broth, turkey, corn, parsley, salt and pepper sauce. Turn up the heat and add pasta when soup begins to boil. Cover and simmer for 10 to 15 minutes, stirring occasionally, until pasta is firm yet tender.

Yield: 9 servings
Per Serving (1 cup):
    166 cal, 2 gm fat, 15 gm pro, 23 gm carb, 25 mg chol,
    688 mg sodium, 3 gm dietary fiber

Canadian Bacon Pizza Soup

The taste of pizza in a soup!

1 (14 1/2 oz.) can chunky pasta-style stewed tomatoes
1 (14 oz.) can chicken broth, defatted
2 c. thinly-sliced zucchini
1 green bell pepper, chopped
2 oz. Canadian bacon, chopped
1 oz. (1/4 c.) reduced-fat Cheddar cheese, shredded
2 oz. (1/2 c.) part-skim mozzarella cheese, shredded

*To defat chicken broth, place can in refrigerator. When cold, skim fat off the top.

1.   In a large saucepan, combine tomatoes, chicken broth, zucchini and bell pepper.
2.   Heat to a boil; reduce heat. Simmer, uncovered, about 5 minutes or until vegetables are tender-crisp.
3.   Stir in Canadian bacon and simmer 1 minute.
4.   Ladle soup into 4 bowls; sprinkle each with 1 tablespoor Cheddar cheese and 2 tablespoons mozzarella cheese.

Yield: 4 servings
Per Serving:

Homemade Chicken Broth

1 onion, cut into wedges
3 celery stalks, cut into 2-inch pieces
3 carrots, cut into 2-inch pieces
2 tsp. dill weed
Bones & skin from 1 small (3 to 3 1/2 lb.) chicken
18 c. water

1. Place all ingredients in a large stockpot and boil for 2 hours.
2. Pour broth through a strainer, discarding all solids.
3. Place broth in jars, filling 3/4-full, and place in refrigerator.
4. When cold, fat will rise to the top. Skim fat off and place broth in freezer for later use.

Yield: 17 cups
Per Serving (1 cup):
    27 cal, 0 gm fat, 5 gm pro, 1 gm carb, 0 mg chol,
    7 mg sodium, 0 gm dietary fiber

Black Bean Chili

The roasted peppers make this dish memorable. Serve with Jalapeño Cornbread and a tossed salad.

1 red bell pepper
1 yellow bell pepper
2 tsp. olive oil
1 c. chopped onion
1 T. ground cumin
1 tsp. chili powder
2 jalapeños, seeded & chopped
4 large garlic cloves, minced
1 (14 1/2 oz.) can chopped tomatoes
1 tsp. oregano
1/4 c. sherry
2 (15 oz.) cans black beans
2 T. chopped cilantro
6 T. light sour cream
Lime wedges (optional)

1. Cut peppers in half lengthwise, removing seeds and stem. Place peppers, skin-side up, under broiler until skins are black. Remove and place in a plastic bag for 10 to 15 minutes. Remove skins and cut into strips.
2. Heat oil in a stockpot and sauté onion for 5 minutes. Add the cumin, chili powder, jalapeños and garlic; cook for another minute.
3. Add tomatoes with liquid, oregano, roasted peppers and sherry; cook over medium heat for 20 minutes. Add black beans with liquid and cook for another 20 to 30 minutes, stirring occasionally. Add a little water to thin if chili becomes too thick.
4. Add cilantro and cook 5 more minutes. Ladle into bowls and top with 1 tablespoon sour cream. Serve with lime wedges.

Yield: 6 servings
Per Serving (~1 1/4 cups):
    212 cal, 4 gm fat, 12 gm pro, 23 gm carb, 5 mg chol,
    769 mg sodium, 10 gm dietary fiber

Sagamity

A Durango, Colorado speciality that warms your tummy.
Serve in a bread bowl.

1 T. olive oil
3 c. chopped onion
2 tsp. minced garlic
2 c. cooked or canned black beans
2 c. cooked or canned pinto beans
2 c. cooked or canned hominy/posole
2 c. frozen corn, defrosted
1 1/2 tsp. chili powder
6 c. spaghetti sauce
1 (14 1/2 oz.) can tomatoes, without added salt
2 T. sherry
1/4 tsp. pepper
1/2 tsp. ground cumin

1. Heat oil in a large saucepan. Add onion and garlic; sauté until onion is transparent.
2. Drain black beans, pinto beans and hominy; rinse off any liquid.
3. Add remaining ingredients and simmer for 30 minutes.

Yield: 12 servings
Per Serving (1 cup):
    232 cal, 5 gm fat, 10 gm pro, 42 gm carb, 0 mg chol,
    453 mg sodium, 8 gm dietary fiber

Chicken Posole

Hominy, a food of the American Indians, is dried white or yellow corn kernels from which the hull and germ have been removed. Dried hominy can be difficult to find. Call Valle Grande Products in Colorado at (303) 936-4274 for your own stash or use 4 3/4 cups canned hominy and reduce the cooking time.

1 1/2 c. dried hominy/posole
6 c. low-sodium chicken broth, defatted*
1 c. chopped onion
2 (4 oz.) cans chopped green chilies
2 tsp. ground cumin
4 garlic cloves, minced
1 tsp. oregano
1 tsp. chili powder
5 (4 oz.) boneless, skinless chicken breasts
2 1/2 oz. (10 T.) reduced-fat Monterey Jack cheese, shredded
Nonfat sour cream (optional)
Chopped cilantro (optional)

*If using canned or homemade chicken broth, place in refrigerator. When cold, skim fat off the top.

1. Place hominy and chicken broth in a large slow-cooker. Cover and soak overnight in refrigerator.
2. Add onion, green chilies, cumin, garlic, oregano, chili powder and chicken. Turn slow-cooker to low and cook for 6 to 7 hours.
3. Stir to break up chicken pieces.
4. Ladle into bowls and top with 2 tablespoons cheese. Add a dollop of sour cream and chopped cilantro, if desired.

Yield: 5 servings
Per Serving:
    329 cal, 7 gm fat, 33 gm pro, 24 gm carb, 80 mg chol,
    540 mg sodium, 6 gm dietary fiber

Notes & Recipes

Entrees

Meat in Your Menu
Herb-Roasted Chicken and Potatoes
Roasted Chicken with Potato, Olive and
Caper Stuffing
Chicken with Tarragon Cream Sauce
Chicken with Apple Pecan Stuffing
Chicken Veronique
Raspberry Chicken
Chicken Parmigiana
Chicken and Tortilla Dumplings
Chicken in the Chips
Edna's Mexican Chicken Casserole
Poblano Peppers with Grilled Chicken
Chicken and Fettuccine Casserole
Turkey Spaghetti
Turkey Pot Pies
Turkey Muffuletta with Tomato Pesto
Steamed Salmon with Fresh Herbs
Salmon with Tarragon Cream Sauce

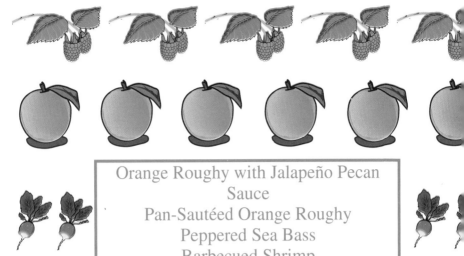

Orange Roughy with Jalapeño Pecan
Sauce
Pan-Sautéed Orange Roughy
Peppered Sea Bass
Barbecued Shrimp
Grilled Shrimp
Oriental Shrimp
Shrimp Enchiladas
Crawfish Casserole
Cowboy Casserole
Beef in Shallot Sauce
Pork Tenderloin with Dijon Mustard
Sauce
Herbed Pork Tenderloin with Maple
Mustard Sauce
Marinated Pork Tenderloin
Garlic-Roasted Pork Loin
Grilled Pork Chops
Hoggle Poggle
Quesadillas with Poblano Pepper
Black Bean Tostadas

Meat in Your Menu

Meat (beef, pork, fish, poultry, etc.) should be the accent of your meals, not the main focus.

For men, keep meat consumption to 6 to 8 ounces per day.

For women, keep meat consumption to 4 to 5 ounces per day.

When consuming beef or pork, choose cuts that have the words loin or round in their name, to ensure that you get a lean, healthy cut. Limit your choice of these lean cuts of beef and pork to 12 ounces per week. Include poultry, fish and meatless meals more often.

Herb-Roasted Chicken and Potatoes

Make an extra chicken for the Herb-Roasted Chicken Salad.

1 small chicken (3 to 3 1/2 lb.)
3 tsp. olive oil, divided use
4 tsp. rosemary, divided use
4 tsp. thyme, divided use
1 tsp. coriander
1 tsp. pepper, divided use
3/4 tsp. salt
1 3/4 lb. small new potatoes
Nonstick vegetable cooking spray

1. Remove neck and organ parts from inside chicken.
2. Rub outside of chicken with 1 teaspoon olive oil.
3. In a small bowl, combine 2 teaspoons rosemary, 2 teaspoons thyme, coriander and 1/2 teaspoon pepper.
4. Place chicken on roasting pan; pat herb mixture onto chicken.
5. Combine remaining 2 teaspoons rosemary, 2 teaspoons thyme, 1/2 teaspoon pepper and salt; set aside.
6. Cut potatoes into quarters. Place in a 9x13-inch baking dish that has been coated with cooking spray.
7. Pour remaining 2 teaspoons olive oil on potatoes and stir until all potatoes are coated.
8. Sprinkle potatoes with herb mixture and stir.
9. Bake chicken and potatoes at 350°F. for 1 hour or until chicken is cooked through. Stir potatoes every 15 minutes.

Yield: 5 servings
Per Serving (chicken without skin):
311 cal, 9 gm fat, 31 gm pro, 24 gm carb, 87 mg chol,
407 mg sodium, 3 gm dietary fiber

Roasted Chicken with Potato, Olive and Caper Stuffing

The combination of rosemary and capers will captivate you.

Chicken:
1 small chicken (3 to 3 1/2 lb.)
1/8 tsp. salt
1/4 tsp. pepper
1 T. fresh or 1 tsp. dried rosemary

Stuffing:
1 1/2 lb. new potatoes, cut into 1-inch pieces
2 T. capers
12 Greek olives, pitted & cut in half
1/3 c. chopped fresh parsley
1 T. minced garlic
1/2 tsp. salt
1/4 tsp. pepper
1 T. fresh or 1 tsp. dried rosemary
2 tsp. olive oil

1. Remove neck and organ parts from inside chicken.
2. Place chicken on roasting pan. Sprinkle outside of chicken with salt, pepper and rosemary; pat so it sticks to chicken.
3. For stuffing, boil potatoes for 15 minutes; drain.
4. Stir remaining stuffing ingredients into potatoes. Stuff chicken. If all of it does not fit, place in a separate covered baking dish.
5. Bake at 350°F. for 1 hour or until chicken is cooked through.

Yield: 5 servings
Per Serving (chicken without skin):
     378 cal, 11 gm fat, 32 gm pro, 38 gm carb, 87 mg chol,
     444 mg sodium, 7 gm dietary fiber

Chicken with Tarragon Cream Sauce

Mmm... Tarragon!

1 small chicken (3 to 3 1/2 lb.)
1/4 tsp. salt, divided use
1/8 tsp. pepper, divided use
3 sprigs plus 2 T. chopped fresh tarragon, divided use
1/2 c. white wine
1 T. Dijon mustard
1/4 c. half & half

1. Remove neck and organ parts from inside chicken.
2. Sprinkle inside of chicken with 1/8 teaspoon salt and dash of pepper. Place 3 sprigs of fresh tarragon inside chicken.
3. Place chicken on roasting pan and bake at 350°F. for 1 hour or until chicken is cooked through.
4. In a small saucepan, heat white wine. Whisk in mustard, half and half and 2 tablespoons tarragon. Cook over low heat, being careful cream does not break. Season with 1/8 teaspoon salt and dash of pepper.
5. Cut up chicken into desired pieces and serve with tarragon cream sauce.

Yield: 5 servings
Per Serving (chicken without skin):
    220 cal, 9 gm fat, 29 gm pro, 1 gm carb, 92 mg chol,
    183 mg sodium, 0 gm dietary fiber

Chicken with Apple Pecan Stuffing

The wonderful aroma this dish creates will call your family to the table before the table is set.

2 Granny Smith apples, chopped
1 c. chopped onion
1/3 c. raisins
3 T. chopped pecans
1 (8 oz.) package cornbread stuffing mix
3/4 tsp. sage
1/4 tsp. salt
1/4 tsp. pepper
1 c. chicken broth
6 skinless chicken breast halves with bone

1. Place all ingredients, except chicken, into a large slow-cooker; stir to combine.
2. Place chicken on top and cook, covered, on low for 6 hours.
3. Remove chicken breasts carefully, using a large spoon or spatula so that bones are not left in the stuffing. Place on a plate and serve with stuffing.

Yield: 6 servings
Per Serving:
    379 cal, 8 gm fat, 32 gm pro, 43 gm carb, 72 mg chol,
    704 mg sodium, 4 gm dietary fiber

Chicken Veronique

Serve on a bed of wild rice with Orange-Glazed Carrots...and enjoy the praise.

Nonstick vegetable cooking spray
1 tsp. margarine
4 (4 oz.) boneless, skinless chicken breasts
1/4 c. dry white wine or sherry
3/4 tsp. tarragon, basil or thyme
1/4 tsp. salt
1/4 c. skim milk
1/3 c. half & half
1 c. seedless green grapes

1. In a skillet coated with cooking spray, heat margarine and brown chicken breasts on both sides.
2. Add wine or sherry, herbs and salt. Cover and simmer for 5 minutes or until chicken is cooked through.
3. Place chicken breasts on a plate and cover to keep warm. Quickly boil pan juices until syrupy. Add skim milk and heat for 1 to 2 minutes. Mix 1 tablespoon of this mixture into half and half. Stir half and half into pan and heat over low heat until slightly thickened, being careful not to let cream break.
4. Stir grapes into cream and cook briefly to heat grapes. Stir in any juices that have drained from the chicken breasts.
5. Place chicken breasts on plates and spoon sauce over them.

Yield: 4 servings
Per Serving:
    208 cal, 6 gm fat, 28 gm pro, 6 gm carb, 80 mg chol,
    224 mg sodium, 0 gm dietary fiber

Raspberry Chicken

Serve this daring dish on Valentines Day for dazzling results.

Nonstick vegetable cooking spray
4 (4 oz.) boneless, skinless chicken breasts
1 tsp. margarine
1/4 c. finely-chopped onions
1/4 c. raspberry vinegar
1/4 c. chicken broth
3/4 T. catsup
1/4 c. half & half
1/4 c. unsweetened frozen raspberries, defrosted

1. In a large skillet that has been coated with cooking spray, melt margarine and add chicken breasts; cook for 2 minutes on each side. Remove and reserve.
2. Add onion to pan and cook until transparent. Add vinegar and cook until the liquid in pan is reduced to about 1 tablespoon. Whisk in chicken broth and catsup. Mix 1 tablespoon of this mixture into half and half and add to pan. Simmer for 2 minutes, being careful that cream does not break.
3. Return chicken to skillet and simmer gently in the sauce, basting until chicken is cooked through, about 5 minutes. Remove chicken to plates and cover to keep warm.
4. Add raspberries to the sauce, breaking them into small pieces with a fork or spatula; cook over low heat for 1 minute.
5. Spoon sauce over chicken.

Yield: 4 servings
Per Serving:
   184 cal, 6 gm fat, 27 gm pro, 4 gm carb, 78 mg chol,
   157 mg sodium, 1 gm dietary fiber

Chicken Parmigiana

The crispy crust provides a believable fat facade.

5 (4 oz.) boneless, skinless chicken breasts
1 egg white
1 1/2 T. water
1 tsp. fresh rosemary
3/4 c. bread crumbs
Nonstick vegetable cooking spray
1/2 T. chopped garlic
1 T. chopped onion
2 c. chopped Roma or plum tomatoes
1 tsp. fresh oregano
1/4 tsp. salt
1/8 tsp. pepper
2 tsp. olive oil
2 1/2 oz. mozzarella cheese, cut into 5 half-slices
2 1/2 T. fresh grated Parmesan cheese

1. Using a meat pounder, pound chicken into thin pieces.
2. In a small bowl, whisk egg white, water and rosemary together.
3. Pour bread crumbs onto a plate.
4. Dip chicken pieces in egg mixture and then coat both sides with bread crumbs. Pat crumbs so they stick.
5. In a small saucepan coated with cooking spray, sauté garlic and onions for 1 minute. Add the tomatoes, oregano, salt and pepper. Bring to a boil and then simmer for 5 minutes.
6. In a large skillet that has been coated with cooking spray, heat remaining 2 teaspoons olive oil and brown chicken on both sides, about 6 minutes total.
7. Place a little of the sauce in a 9x13-inch baking dish. Add the chicken and cover with more sauce. Place 1/2 slice mozzarella cheese on each piece and then cover with remaining sauce. Sprinkle with Parmesan cheese.
8. Bake at 400°F. for 10 minutes or until cheese is melted.

Yield: 5 servings
Per Serving:
    299 cal, 10 gm fat, 35 gm pro, 15 gm carb, 83 mg chol,
    448 mg sodium, 2 gm dietary fiber

Chicken and Tortilla Dumplings

Keep the name a secret, your family and friends will never guess that the "dumplings" are actually tortillas.

Nonstick vegetable cooking spray
3/4 c. chopped onion
3 carrots, sliced
5 c. low-sodium chicken broth, defatted*
3 (4 oz.) boneless, skinless chicken breasts
12 corn tortillas, cut into small strips
3/4 c. skim milk
1/4 tsp. pepper
1/4 tsp. thyme
1/2 T. parsley
3/4 tsp. salt

*If using homemade or canned chicken broth, defat by placing in refrigerator. When cold, skim fat off the top.

1. In a large saucepan coated with cooking spray, sauté onion until transparent.
2. Add carrots and chicken broth and boil for 10 minutes.
3. Add chicken and cook for 5 to 10 minutes until chicken is cooked through.
4. Remove chicken and add tortillas to broth mixture. Cook, covered, on low for 15 minutes.
5. Cut chicken into bite-size pieces and add to mixture along with milk, pepper, thyme, parsley and salt.
6. Cook for a few more minutes to heat milk, then ladle into bowls.

Yield: 5 servings
Per Serving:
    265 cal, 4 gm fat, 21 gm pro, 33 gm carb, 44 mg chol,
    578 mg sodium, 5 gm dietary fiber

Chicken in the Chips

The original version included fat-filled corn chips; the baked chips provide the crunch without all the fat.

5 (4 oz.) boneless, skinless chicken breasts
1 (10 3/4 oz.) can reduced-sodium, reduced-fat cream of chicken
    soup
1/2 c. nonfat sour cream
2 T. picante sauce
4 oz. (1 c.) reduced-fat Monterey Jack cheese, shredded, divided
    use
1 c. chopped onion
1 tomato, chopped
1 Anaheim or poblano pepper, chopped
1 1/2 oz. baked tortilla chips

1. Place chicken breasts in boiling water and cook for 5 to 10 minutes until cooked through. Cut into bite-size pieces.
2. Combine chicken, soup, sour cream, picante sauce, 1/2 cup cheese, onion, tomato and Anaheim pepper.
3. Pour mixture into a 9x13-inch casserole dish. Top with remaining 1/2 cup cheese.
4. Crush all but 6 chips. Sprinkle top with crushed ones and stick whole chips in 1/2 way.
5. Bake at 350°F. for 20 to 30 minutes, until bubbly.

Yield: 6 servings
Per Serving:
    263 cal, 7 gm fat, 31 gm pro, 16 gm carb, 75 mg chol,
    493 mg sodium, 2 gm dietary fiber

Edna's Mexican Chicken Casserole

Serve with a green salad and black beans as suggested by Edna Ground.

8 (4 oz.) boneless, skinless chicken breasts
1 tsp. margarine
1 c. chopped onion
12 oz. Velveeta Light cheese, cut into 1-inch cubes
1/2 c. picante sauce
1 (10 3/4 oz.) can reduced-sodium, reduced-fat cream of mush-
    room soup
1 c. skim milk
1 lb. frozen broccoli with corn and red peppers
6 c. (11 oz.) crushed, baked tortilla chips*

*To further reduce sodium, use 1/2 unsalted baked chips.

1. Place chicken in boiling water and cook for 5 to 10 minutes until
    cooked through. Remove and cut into bite-size pieces.
2. In a skillet, heat margarine and sauté onion until transparent.
3. Place cheese and picante sauce in a covered dish and micro-
    wave until melted (4 to 6 minutes), stirring once or twice during
    cooking.
4. Add onion, soup and milk to cheese mixture and heat in
    microwave until blended (about 3 minutes).
5. Place frozen vegetables in a covered dish and microwave for 5
    minutes.
6. Mix chicken, sauce, vegetables and chips together.
7. Pour mixture into a 9x13-inch baking dish and bake at 350°F.
    for 15 to 20 minutes, until hot.

Yield: 12 servings
Per Serving:
    307 cal, 7 gm fat, 29 gm pro, 31 gm carb, 59 mg chol,
    771 mg sodium, 3 gm dietary fiber

Poblano Peppers with Grilled Chicken

A remake of an authentic Mexican dish.

4 poblano peppers
4 (4 oz.) boneless, skinless chicken breasts, grilled & thinly sliced
1/2 c. chopped cilantro
3 oz. (3/4 c.) reduced-fat Monterey Jack cheese, shredded

1. Make a lengthwise slit in peppers and remove seeds. Place peppers under broiler until skin is barely black. Turn over and repeat.
2. Place peppers, slit-side up, in a baking dish. Stuff with chicken and cilantro; top with cheese.
3. Bake at 350°F. for 15 minutes.

Yield: 4 servings
Per Serving:
    212 cal, 7 gm fat, 34 gm pro, 2 gm carb, 87 mg chol,
    230 mg sodium, 2 gm dietary fiber

Chicken and Fettuccine Casserole

Serve with a green salad.

1 T. margarine
1/4 c. flour
1 c. skim milk
1 c. chicken broth
4 (4 oz.) boneless, skinless chicken breasts
8 oz. dried fettuccine, cooked according to package directions,
    omitting salt & fat
1 c. nonfat sour cream
1 c. nonfat plain yogurt
1 (10 oz.) package frozen, chopped spinach, cooked & drained
    well
1 (6 oz.) jar sliced mushrooms, drained
1 (8 oz.) can sliced water chestnuts, drained
1 (4 oz.) jar pimentos, drained
1/2 c. chopped onions
1/2 c. chopped celery
1/3 c. lemon juice
2 tsp. Knorr Seasoning for Meat
1/2 tsp. cayenne pepper
1 tsp. paprika
1/2 tsp. pepper
4 oz. (1 c.) reduced-fat Monterey Jack cheese, shredded

1. Place chicken in boiling water and cook for 5 to 10 minutes until chicken is cooked through. Remove and cut into bite-size pieces.
2. In a small saucepan, melt margarine. Stir in flour.
3. Add milk and chicken broth; cook, stirring continuously, until thickened. Mixture may be a little lumpy.
4. In a large bowl, combine milk mixture with all ingredients, except cheese; stir well. Pour into a 9x13-inch casserole dish and top with cheese.
6. Bake for 25 to 30 minutes at 300°F.

Yield: 10 servings
Per Serving:
    276 cal, 6 gm fat, 23 gm pro, 32 gm carb, 38 mg chol,
    627 mg sodium, 2 gm dietary fiber

Turkey Spaghetti

Make this the day after Thanksgiving to get back on the low-fat track.

1 tsp. olive oil
1 c. chopped onion
3 stalks celery, chopped
1 (4 oz.) can sliced mushrooms, drained
12 oz. dried spaghetti, cooked according to package directions,
    omitting salt & fat
12 oz. (2 1/3 c.) chopped, cooked turkey without skin
2 (10 3/4 oz.) cans reduced-sodium, reduced-fat cream of
    chicken soup
1/2 c. skim milk
1/4 tsp. pepper
3/4 tsp. garlic powder
4 oz. (1 c.) reduced-fat Cheddar cheese, shredded

1. In a small skillet, heat oil. Sauté onion and celery in oil until
    onion is slightly transparent.
2. In a large bowl, combine onions and celery with all remaining
    ingredients except cheese.
3. Place mixture in a 9x13-inch casserole dish and top with cheese.
4. Bake at 350°F. for 30 minutes.

Yield: 9 servings
Per Serving:
    290 cal, 7 gm fat, 21 gm pro, 36 gm carb, 38 mg chol,
    461 mg sodium, 2 gm dietary fiber

Turkey Pot Pies

Freezes well. Wrap in plastic wrap, then foil. Defrost in the refrigerator 24 hours and then bake as directed.

1 1/2 plus 2/3 c. flour
1/4 tsp. salt
3 T. margarine
4 oz. fat-free cream cheese
1 to 2 T. water
4 c. chicken broth, defatted*
1 c. thinly-sliced carrots
8 oz. sliced mushrooms
2/3 c. flour
1/2 c. evaporated skim milk
3 c. cooked turkey without skin, cut into small pieces
1 c. frozen peas, defrosted
1/4 c. chopped fresh parsley
1/4 tsp. pepper

*If using homemade or canned chicken broth, place in refrigerator. When cold, skim fat off the top. To reduce sodium further, use low-sodium chicken broth.

1. To make pastry, combine 1 1/2 cups flour and salt. Cut in margarine and cream cheese, using a food processor or pastry blender, until mixture resembles cornmeal (if using a pastry blender, first cut margarine and cream cheese into small bits). Add 1 tablespoon water and stir with a fork. Add up to 1 tablespoon more water to make a cohesive dough. Form into a small ball. Wrap in plastic wrap and chill 1 hour.
2. Bring chicken broth to a boil in a large saucepan. Add carrots and mushrooms; cover and simmer 15 minutes until vegetables are tender.

Continued on following page.

Continued from preceding page.

3. Strain broth, reserving vegetables. Add enough water to broth to make 4 cups; reserve.
4. Wipe inside of saucepan with a paper towel. Add 2/3 cup flour and brown it over low heat, stirring constantly. Add broth mixture to flour and bring to a boil, stirring constantly. Reduce heat; add evaporated skim milk and simmer 2 minutes. Stir in the turkey, carrots, mushrooms, peas, parsley and pepper.
5. Divide the filling among 6 ovenproof dishes or 6 (4-inch) aluminum pie pans.
6. Roll out pastry on floured surface and cut 6 circles 1-inch larger than top of dishes. Lay pastry over filling and crimp the edges. Cut vents in top and place on a baking sheet. Bake at 425°F. for 20 to 25 minutes, until browned and bubbling.

Yield: 6 servings
Per Serving:
    420 cal, 10 gm fat, 35 gm pro, 45 gm carb, 58 mg chol,
    903 mg sodium, 4 gm dietary fiber

Turkey Muffuletta with Tomato Pesto

The foil wrapping makes it a convenient take-with-you entree.

1/2 c. sun-dried tomatoes
1/2 c. hot water
1/4 c. Greek or other black olives, pitted
2 tsp. olive oil
2 garlic cloves
1 tsp. anchovy paste
2 T. fresh parsley
3 T. fresh basil
1/4 tsp. pepper
1 (1 lb.) round loaf of bread
8 oz. cooked turkey breast, thinly sliced
4 oz. part-skim mozzarella cheese, thinly sliced

1. Soak sun-dried tomatoes in hot water for 10 to 15 minutes until soft; drain.
2. Place tomatoes, olives, olive oil, garlic, anchovy paste, parsley, basil and pepper in food processor and process until pureed.
3. Slice bread in half horizontally. Spread both sides with tomato pesto and arrange turkey and cheese on bottom half. Place other half on top and wrap entire sandwich in foil.
4. Bake at 350°F. for 20 to 30 minutes, until cheese is melted and sandwich is hot.
5. Cut into 8 wedges and serve hot or warm.

Yield: 8 servings
Per Serving (1 wedge):
    270 cal, 7 gm fat, 18 gm pro, 32 gm carb, 27 mg chol,
    452 mg sodium, 1 gm dietary fiber

Steamed Salmon with Fresh Herbs

Cooking in foil is very easy. No mess. Serve with Penny's Roasted Vegetables.

8 oz. salmon fillets
1/8 tsp. lemon peel
2 sprigs (~2 T.) fresh tarragon, dill weed or basil
2 T. white wine

1. Cut salmon into 2 pieces and lay each on a piece of aluminum foil measuring 12x12 inches.
2. Sprinkle with lemon pepper and lay herbs on top.
3. Fold sides of foil up halfway and add white wine. Fold foil, sealing all edges and allowing a pocket of space over salmon.
4. Bake at 400°F. for 10 to 12 minutes, until salmon is cooked through.

Yield: 2 servings
Per Serving:
    173 cal, 7 gm fat, 22 gm pro, 1 gm carb, 60 mg chol,
    50 mg sodium, 0 gm dietary fiber

Salmon with Tarragon Cream Sauce

The tarragon adds the French flair without the fat.

Nonstick vegetable cooking spray
8 oz. sliced mushrooms
1 1/2 c. white wine
4 (4 oz.) salmon fillets
2 T. skim milk
2 T. fresh tarragon
1/3 c. half & half
1/4 tsp. salt
1/8 tsp. pepper

1. In a skillet that has been coated with cooking spray, sauté mushrooms just until tender. Transfer mushrooms and juice to a bowl and set aside.
2. Pour wine into the skillet and bring to a boil. Reduce heat and add the salmon. Cover and poach fish until opaque throughout when tested with a knife, about 8 minutes. If fish is thick, you may need to turn it over to cook it through.
3. Using a slotted spatula, transfer salmon to a warmed platter and cover to keep warm.
4. Increase heat and reduce the pan juices to a syrupy glaze, about 5 to 8 minutes.
5. Reduce heat and stir in the reserved mushrooms with their juice, milk and tarragon; cook for 1 to 2 minutes. Stir 1 tablespoon of this mixture into half and half and add to pan. Simmer for 1 more minute, being careful that cream does not break. Season with salt and pepper.
6. Spoon mushroom sauce over the salmon and serve immediately.

Yield: 4 servings
Per serving:
  261 cal, 10 gm fat, 24 gm pro, 5 gm carb, 68 mg chol,
  202 mg sodium, 1 gm fiber

Orange Roughy with Jalapeño Pecan Sauce

A wonderful Southern dish.

Nonstick vegetable cooking spray
4 (5 oz.) orange roughy fillets
1 1/2 tsp. melted margarine
1 jalapeño pepper, stem & seeds removed
1 garlic clove
2 T. pecans
2 T. cilantro
1/8 tsp. salt

1. Coat a broiler pan with cooking spray. Place fish on prepared pan and coat top with cooking spray. Broil for 3 to 5 minutes*.
2. In a food processor, combine margarine, jalapeño pepper, garlic, pecans, cilantro and salt. Process until smooth.
3. Spread sauce over fish and place under broiler for an additional 3 to 5 minutes*.

* Cooking time will depend on thickness of fish. Broil for a total of 10 minutes per 1-inch thickness of fish.

Yield: 4 servings
Per Serving:
    132 cal, 5 gm fat, 20 gm pro, 1 gm carb, 28 mg chol,
    221 mg sodium, 0 gm dietary fiber

Pan-Sautéed Orange Roughy

1 lb. orange roughy
1 1/2 tsp. lemon pepper
1/2 to 1 tsp. garlic powder
1/8 tsp. salt
2 T. flour
Nonstick vegetable cooking spray
2 tsp. olive oil

1. Sprinkle fish with lemon pepper, garlic powder (to taste) and salt. Lightly coat with flour.
2. In a skillet coated with cooking spray, heat oil. Add fish and sauté until flaky (about 5 minutes), turning once.

Yield: 4 servings
Per Serving:
   114 cal, 3 gm fat, 17 gm pro, 4 gm carb, 22 mg chol,
   263 mg sodium, 0 gm dietary fiber

Peppered Sea Bass

The decoration of peppers atop the bass makes an impressive dish.

6 Roma or plum tomatoes, seeded
8 fresh basil leaves, divided use
3 garlic cloves
1 jalapeño, stem & seeds removed
2 T. fresh parsley
2 tsp. olive oil, divided use
2 tsp. balsamic vinegar
1/4 tsp. salt
1/4 tsp. pepper, divided use
1 red bell pepper
1 yellow bell pepper
4 (4 oz.) sea bass steaks

1. To make sauce, place tomatoes, 4 basil leaves, garlic, jalapeño, parsley, 1 teaspoon olive oil, vinegar, salt and 1/8 teaspoon pepper in a food processor or blender. Process until smooth. Pour into a small saucepan.
2. Cut bell peppers in half lengthwise, and remove stem and seeds. Place under broiler, skin-side up, until black. Remove and place in plastic bag for 10 to 15 minutes. Remove skins from peppers and cut into small strips.
3. Brush sea bass with remaining teaspoon of olive oil and sprinkle with remaining pepper. Bake at 400°F. for 10 minutes per 1-inch thickness of fish. Heat sauce while fish is cooking.
4. Place 1/4 of tomato sauce on each plate, making a puddle. Place fish in middle and top with roasted pepper strips. Place additional basil leaves on top of peppers.

Yield: 4 servings
Per Serving:
    139 cal, 5 gm fat, 17 gm pro, 8 gm carb, 68 mg chol,
    206 mg sodium, 2 gm dietary fiber

Barbecued Shrimp

Ladle into bowls and serve with crusty French bread to soak up the sauce.

1 lb. medium (36 to 40 count) shrimp
1/2 T. canola oil
2 tsp. margarine, melted
2 T. lemon juice
1/4 c. white wine
1 T. Worcestershire sauce
1 T. parsley
1 tsp. pepper
1 1/2 tsp. minced garlic
1/2 tsp. Knorr Seasoning for Meat
1/2 tsp. lemon pepper
1/4 tsp. hot pepper sauce

1. Rinse and drain shrimp. Place in a baking dish large enough so they can fit in one layer.
2. Mix together the remaining ingredients and pour over shrimp.
3. Bake at 400°F. for 20 minutes, stirring twice.

Yield: 4 servings
Per Serving (9 to 10 shrimp with sauce):
    136 cal, 5 gm fat, 18 gm pro, 2 gm carb, 166 mg chol,
    470 mg sodium, 0 gm dietary fiber

Grilled Shrimp

1 lb. medium (36 to 40 count) shrimp, peeled & deveined
1/2 T. olive oil
1/2 T. canola oil
1/4 c. bread crumbs
1 garlic clove, minced
1 T. chopped Italian parsley

1. In a bowl, toss shrimp and oil.
2. Add bread crumbs and toss lightly.
3. Add garlic and parsley; toss lightly again.
4. Refrigerate for 2 hours.
5. Put on skewers and grill until pink.

Yield: 4 servings
Per Serving (9 to 10 shrimp):
    143 cal, 5 gm fat, 19 gm pro, 5 gm carb, 166 mg chol,
    238 mg sodium, 0 gm dietary fiber

Oriental Shrimp

Eat with chopsticks.

1 1/2 lb. medium (36 to 40 count) shrimp
1/2 c. brown sugar, firmly packed
1/2 c. vinegar
3/4 tsp. salt
1/2 tsp. ginger
1 tsp. light soy sauce
2 1/2 T. cornstarch
1 (8 oz.) can pineapple chunks in juice, drained, juice reserved
1 (11 oz.) can mandarin oranges in light syrup, drained
1 green bell pepper, cut into small strips
4 tomatoes, cut into wedges
1/2 c. chopped onion
1 c. sliced mushrooms
3 c. cooked rice

1. Place shrimp in a pot of boiling water and cook just until water comes back to a boil. Drain water and cool shrimp in refrigerator.
2. Peel and devein shrimp.
3. In a large skillet, combine brown sugar, vinegar, salt, ginger and soy sauce.
4. In a small bowl, combine cornstarch with reserved pineapple juice. Stir into mixture in skillet.
5. Add all remaining ingredients except shrimp and rice. Bring to a boil; reduce heat and simmer, covered, for 15 minutes.
6. Add shrimp and cook for 1 to 2 minutes to heat shrimp. Serve over rice.

Yield: 6 servings
Per Serving:
    367 cal, 2 gm fat, 22 gm pro, 64 carb, 166 mg chol,
    554 mg sodium, 3 gm dietary fiber

Shrimp Enchiladas

Stop by your favorite Mexican eatery for fresh homemade corn tortillas.

1 lb. medium shrimp (36 to 40 count)
1 tsp. margarine
1 1/2 c. chopped onion
1/2 tsp. ground cumin
2 (7 oz.) cans green salsa
12 corn tortillas
3 oz. (3/4 c.) reduced-fat Monterey Jack cheese, shredded
Nonstick vegetable cooking spray
1 c. skim milk
1 c. light sour cream
Paprika, to taste

1. Place shrimp in a pot of boiling water and cook just until water comes back to a boil. Drain water and cool shrimp in refrigerator.
2. In a skillet, heat margarine. Add onion and sauté until transparent.
3. Stir in cumin and salsa verda and cook for a few minutes.
4. Peel and devein shrimp.
5. Dip tortillas in onion mixture, coating both sides. Place 3 to 4 shrimp and 1 tablespoon cheese in each one. Roll up the tortillas and place, seam-side down, in a 9x13-inch baking dish that has been coated with cooking spray*.
6. Pour remaining onion mixture, then skim milk, over the top.
7. Bake at 350°F. for 20 minutes.
8. Heat sour cream in a saucepan just until hot.
9. Place enchiladas on plates. Spoon sour cream over the top and sprinkle with paprika.

*If tortillas are difficult to roll, heat in microwave before or after dipping in sauce.

Yield: 6 servings
Per Serving (2 enchiladas):
    297 cal, 9 gm fat, 24 gm pro, 30 gm carb, 132 mg chol,
    826 mg sodium, 4 gm dietary fiber

Crawfish Casserole

A Louisiana treat that brings you back to the bayou.

1 tsp. canola oil
1 c. chopped onion
1/2 c. chopped green bell pepper
1 c. chopped celery
1 lb. crawfish meat or peeled & deveined shrimp
1 (10 3/4 oz.) can reduced-sodium, reduced-fat cream of mush-
    room soup
1/3 c. water
1 (4 oz.) jar pimentos
1/3 c. chopped fresh parsley
1/2 c. chopped green onions
2 1/2 c. cooked rice
1/4 tsp. pepper
1 1/2 tsp. Tony Chachere's Creole Seasoning
1/3 c. bread crumbs
1 T. margarine, cut into small pieces

1. In a large skillet, heat oil and sauté onion, pepper and celery until onion is transparent. Add crawfish or shrimp and simmer for 5 minutes.
2. Place crawfish mixture in a large bowl and add soup, water, pimentos, parsley, green onions, rice, pepper and Creole Seasoning; stir well.
3. Pour into a 9x13-inch baking dish. Top with bread crumbs and dot with margarine.
4. Bake at 325°F. for 30 minutes.

Yield: 6 servings
Per Serving:
    266 cal, 5 gm fat, 17 gm pro, 35 gm carb, 88 mg chol,
    759 mg sodium, 2 gm dietary fiber

Cowboy Casserole

A pleasing meal for the cowboys in your life.

1 1/2 c. cornmeal
1/2 c. flour
1 T. baking powder
1 T. sugar
1/2 tsp. salt
3 egg whites or 6 T. egg substitute
1 1/2 tsp. canola oil, divided use
1 c. buttermilk
1 (4 oz.) can chopped green chilies
Nonstick vegetable cooking spray
1 lb. 90% lean ground beef
1 green bell pepper, chopped
1 c. chopped onion
1 1/2 c. cooked or canned pinto beans, drained & rinsed of bean
    liquid
2 (10 oz.) cans tomatoes with green chilies, drained & chopped
1 1/2 tsp. chili powder
2 T. ground cumin
1/8 tsp. pepper
3/4 c. chopped cilantro
4 oz. (1 c.) reduced-fat Monterey Jack cheese, shredded
1/4 c. chopped green onions

1. In a bowl, stir cornmeal, flour, baking powder, sugar and salt
    together.
2. In a separate bowl, whisk egg whites or egg substitute, 1/2
    teaspoon oil and buttermilk together. Add to the flour mixture
    and stir just until combined.
3. Fold in green chilies.
4. Pour half of batter into a 9x13-inch baking dish that has been
    coated with cooking spray. Bake at 325°F. for 20 minutes or
    until barely firm.

Continued on following page.

Continued from preceding page.

5. Cook ground beef in skillet or microwave until browned; drain and set aside.
6. In a large skillet, heat remaining 1 teaspoon oil and sauté the green peppers and onions until onions are transparent.
7. Add the cooked ground beef, pinto beans, tomatoes, chili powder, cumin and pepper to the onion mixture; stir until well mixed.
8. Spread this mixture over the baked cornbread and sprinkle with cilantro.
9. Spread the remaining cornbread batter over the top and sprinkle with cheese and green onions. Bake at 325°F. for 30 minutes or until firm.

Yield: 8 servings
Per Serving:
364 cal, 9 gm fat, 26 gm pro, 39 gm carb, 47 mg chol,
780 mg sodium, 6 gm dietary fiber

Beef in Shallot Sauce

A special occasion meal. Plan this meal when you have had a meatless lunch.

Nonstick vegetable cooking spray
3 (6 oz.) fillet mignon (tenderloin) or sirloin steaks
1/8 tsp. pepper
2 T. chopped shallots
1/3 c. red wine
1/2 c. beef broth
1 tsp. margarine
1 tsp. flour

1. Place steaks in skillet that has been coated with cooking spray. Brown on both sides, cooking until desired doneness. Sprinkle with pepper and keep warm on heated platter or in oven.
2. Add shallots to skillet and sauté for 2 minutes. Add wine and stir to loosen solids. Simmer and reduce liquid to half.
3. Add beef broth and reduce by half again.
4. Strain sauce, discarding solids, and return liquid to skillet.
5. Whisk in margarine and flour; continue cooking, stirring constantly, until sauce has thickened.
6. Place meat on plate and spoon sauce over top.

Yield: 3 servings
Per Serving (without bacon, if fillets were wrapped in bacon):
330 cal, 17 gm fat, 37 gm pro, 2 gm carb, 110 mg chol,
352 mg sodium, 0 gm dietary fiber

Pork Tenderloin with Dijon Mustard Sauce

Don't be fooled by the rich color of the sauce, it's nearly guilt-free.

2 lb. pork tenderloin
1 1/2 T. rosemary
2 tsp. oregano
1/4 tsp. salt, divided use
2 T. egg substitute
1 T. Dijon mustard
1/4 c. half & half
2 tsp. olive oil
1/2 c. white wine
1/8 tsp. pepper
1/2 tsp. sherry
1 garlic clove, minced
1 tsp. tarragon

1. Place pork on roasting pan and sprinkle with rosemary, oregano and 1/8 teaspoon salt, patting lightly so herbs stick to meat.
2. Bake in oven at 375°F. for 45 minutes to 1 hour, until internal temperature of meat reaches 170°F.
3. In a small bowl, whisk egg substitute and mustard together. Stir in half and half; set aside.
4. In a small saucepan, combine olive oil, wine, 1/8 teaspoon salt, pepper, sherry, garlic and tarragon; boil for 1 minute.
5. Reduce heat and stir in cream mixture. Stir over low heat just until thickened, being careful that cream does not break.
6. Slice meat and serve with sauce.

Yield: 8 servings
Per Serving (3 ounces of meat with sauce):
    196 cal, 8 gm fat, 27 gm pro, 1 gm carb, 83 mg chol,
    156 mg sodium, 0 gm dietary fiber

Herbed Pork Tenderloin with Maple Mustard Sauce

Serve with Roasted Potatoes and Green Beans.

1 lb. pork tenderloin
1 T. herbs de Provence*
1/4 c. maple syrup
1/4 c. Dijon mustard

*Herbs de Provence may be found in the spice section of your grocery store, or make your own with the Herbs de Provence recipe included in this book.

1. Place pork on roasting pan and sprinkle with herbs, patting lightly so they stick to meat.
2. Bake in oven at 375°F. for 45 minutes to 1 hour, until internal temperature of meat reaches 170°F.
3. Whisk together syrup and mustard; let it reach room temperature while meat is cooking.
4. Slice meat and serve with sauce on the side.

Yield: 4 servings
Per Serving (3 ounces of meat with 2 tablespoons of sauce):
225 cal, 6 gm fat, 27 gm pro, 14 gm carb, 80 mg chol,
245 mg sodium, 1 gm dietary fiber

Marinated Pork Tenderloin

Make it once and you'll make it for a lifetime.

1/2 tsp. ginger
1/2 onion
2 garlic cloves
2 tsp. basil
1 1/2 tsp. parsley
3 T. light soy sauce
1 T. canola oil
2 lb. pork tenderloin

1. Combine all ingredients except tenderloin. Process in food processor or blender until well mixed.
2. Pour over pork tenderloin. Marinate in refrigerator for 1 hour or overnight.
3. Grill over hot coals or gas grill, low to medium heat, or bake in oven at 350°F. for 30 to 45 minutes. Meat is done when internal temperature reaches 170°F.

Yield: 8 servings
Per Serving (3 ounces of meat):
    171 cal, 6 gm fat, 26 gm pro, 1 gm carb, 80 mg chol,
    165 mg sodium, 0 gm dietary fiber

Garlic-Roasted Pork Loin

Due to its ease of preparation and duration of cooking, this trusted main entree allows you to experiment with some of our unique side dishes.

1 1/2 lb. pork loin roast
1 tsp. garlic powder
1 T. rosemary
1/4 tsp. salt
1/4 tsp. pepper

1. Cover roast with seasonings, patting to help seasonings stick.
2. Bake at 350°F. for 1 1/2 to 2 hours, until internal temperature of meat reaches 170°F.

Yield: 6 servings
Per Serving:
    196 cal, 10 gm fat, 25 gm pro, 1 gm carb, 66 mg chol,
    128 mg sodium, 0 gm dietary fiber

Grilled Pork Chops

A good meat to grill in the summer.

4 (4 oz.) pork loin chops
4 T. light teriyaki sauce

1. Place chops in a pan and drizzle with teriyaki sauce. Marinate in refrigerator for 2 hours, turning chops 2 to 3 times to coat with marinade.
2. Grill over hot coals or gas grill, low to medium heat. Chops are done when internal temperature reaches 170°F.

Yield: 4 servings
Per Serving (1 chop):
    180 cal, 8 gm fat, 24 gm pro, 2 gm carb, 67 mg chol,
    296 mg sodium, 0 gm dietary fiber

Hoggle Poggle

It's a whole-meal deal.

1 1/2 lb. potatoes
1/2 T. margarine
2 green onions, chopped
3/4 c. frozen peas
1/8 tsp. pepper
1/4 tsp. paprika
1/8 tsp. seasoned salt
4 oz. lean baked ham*

*Choose ham with 5 grams of fat per 3 ounces.

1. Peel potatoes and cut into 1-inch pieces. Boil until tender.
2. In a medium skillet, melt margarine. Add all ingredients except ham. Cook over medium-high heat, turning potatoes so that all of them are browned.
3. Add ham and cook a few more minutes.

Yield: 2 servings
Per Serving:
366 cal, 6 gm fat, 21 gm pro, 56 gm carb, 30 mg chol, 855 mg sodium, 8 gm dietary fiber

Quesadillas with Poblano Pepper

Nonstick vegetable cooking spray
4 (6-inch) wholewheat flour tortillas, made without lard
1 1/2 oz. (6 T.) reduced-fat Monterey Jack cheese, shredded
1/3 c. chopped poblano pepper
1/4 c. chopped cilantro

1. Spray a large (or 2 small) skillet with cooking spray. Place 2 tortillas flat in skillet.
2. Place 1/2 of cheese, poblano peppers and cilantro on each tortilla; place remaining 2 tortillas on top.
3. Cook on medium heat until bottom of tortillas are lightly browned. Flip quesadillas and brown other sides.
4. Cut each quesadilla into 4 pieces and serve.

Yield: 2 servings
Per Serving (4 pieces):
    236 cal, 8 gm fat, 12 gm pro, 31 gm carb, 15 mg chol,
    477 mg sodium, 7 gm dietary fiber

Black Bean Tostadas

Lots of dietary fiber in this easy Mexican recipe.

4 corn tortillas
Nonstick vegetable cooking spray
1 c. cooked or canned black beans, drained & rinsed of bean liquid
1 oz. (1/4 c.) reduced-fat Monterey Jack cheese, shredded
4 T. picante sauce
1 tomato, chopped
1/4 c. chopped cilantro

1. Place tortillas on cookie sheet that has been coated with cooking spray. Bake at 350°F. for 10 minutes until tortillas are crispy.
2. Top tortillas with beans, cheese, picante sauce, tomato and cilantro.
3. Return to oven and bake for 5 to 10 minutes until cheese is melted.

Yield: 2 servings
Per Serving (2 tostadas):
    301 cal, 6 gm fat, 16 gm pro, 38 gm carb, 8 mg chol,
    193 mg sodium, 11 gm dietary fiber

Meatless Meals

Black Bean Chili

Sagamity

Tomato Basil Pasta with Pine Nuts

Bow Tie Pasta with Blue Cheese

Red and Green Pasta

Penne Pasta with Feta Cheese and Sun-Dried Tomatoes

Baked Penne Pasta with Tomato Basil Sauce

Sun-Dried Tomato and Feta Cheese Pizza

Pesto and Cheddar Pizza

Mexican Pizza

Risotto with Sun-Dried Tomatoes and Mozzarella Cheese

Risotto with Blue Cheese

Primavera Sauce
(served over pasta)

Pesto Sauce
(served with pasta)

Pastas and Pizzas

Tomato Basil Pasta with Pine Nuts
Angel Hair Pasta with Shrimp in Roasted Pepper Cream Sauce
Bow Tie Pasta with Blue Cheese
Red and Green Pasta
Penne Pasta with Feta Cheese and Sun-Dried Tomatoes
Chicken and Zucchini in Tomato Sauce
Fettuccine with Chicken and Asparagus
Baked Penne Pasta with Tomato Basil Sauce
Mo's Great Lasagna
White Lasagna with Canadian Bacon
Lasagna with Grilled Chicken and Pesto
Canadian Bacon Pizza
Sun-Dried Tomato and Feta Cheese Pizza

Barbecued Chicken Pizza

Pesto and Cheddar Pizza

Mexican Pizza

Risotto with Sun-Dried Tomatoes and
Mozzarella Cheese

Seafood Risotto

Risotto with Blue Cheese

Primavera Sauce

Pesto Sauce

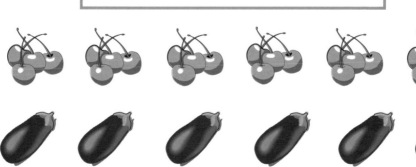

Tomato Basil Pasta with Pine Nuts

Simple sauce, the pine nuts add the finishing touch.

6 oz. dried penne pasta
2 tsp. olive oil
4 Roma or 2 regular tomatoes, chopped
1 tsp. minced garlic
1/4 c. chopped fresh basil
1/4 tsp. salt
Dash of pepper
2 T. fresh grated Parmesan cheese
1 tsp. parsley
1 1/2 T. pine nuts, toasted*

*To toast pine nuts, place under broiler just until lightly browned and fragrant. This takes just a couple of minutes, so watch them carefully!

1. Cook pasta according to package directions, omitting salt and fat.
2. In a saucepan, heat olive oil. Add tomatoes, garlic and basil; cook over medium heat for 6 to 7 minutes. Season with salt and pepper.
3. Pour tomato mixture over pasta and stir to combine.
4. Divide among 3 plates and top with cheese, parsley and pine nuts.

Yield: 3 servings
Per Serving:
    284 cal, 7 gm fat, 10 gm pro, 45 gm carb, 3 mg chol,
    251 mg sodium, 3 gm dietary fiber

Angel Hair Pasta with Shrimp in Roasted Pepper Cream Sauce

Jalapeño hot!

1 lb. medium shrimp (36 to 40 count)
4 to 8 fresh jalapeño peppers
2 red bell peppers
1 lb. dried angel hair pasta
1 c. skim milk
1 c. half & half
1/2 tsp. salt
1/8 tsp. pepper (optional)

1. Place shrimp in a pan of boiling water and cook just until water comes back to a boil; drain. Place in refrigerator to cool.
2. Peel and devein shrimp.
3. Cut jalapeño and red bell peppers in half lengthwise, removing seeds and stem. Place peppers, skin-side up, under broiler until skins are black. Remove and place in a plastic bag for 10 to 15 minutes. Remove skins and cut into small pieces*.
4. Cook pasta according to package directions, omitting salt and fat; drain well.
5. While pasta is cooking, heat milk in a small saucepan along with red peppers and half of jalapeño peppers, until milk is hot, but not boiling.
6. Mix 2 tablespoons of milk mixture into half and half. Slowly stir half and half into pan, being careful not to let cream break.
7. Add shrimp and salt; continue to cook over low heat for just a few minutes.
8. Taste sauce and add more jalapeño peppers and black pepper according to desired intensity.

*Use plastic gloves while handling jalapeño peppers to avoid burning your skin.

Yield: 6 servings
Per Serving:
    379 cal, 6 gm fat, 19 gm pro, 59 gm carb, 72 mg chol,
    305 mg sodium, 3 gm dietary fiber

Bow Tie Pasta with Blue Cheese

Easy as 1, 2, 3.

8 oz. dried bow tie (farfalle) pasta
3 oz. blue cheese
1/3 c. skim milk
2 T. fresh grated Parmesan cheese
4 tsp. parsley

1. Cook pasta according to package directions, omitting salt and fat.
2. Crumble blue cheese over pasta and add skim milk; stir until cheese is melted.
3. Divide between 4 plates; top with Parmesan cheese and parsley.

Yield: 4 servings
Per Serving:
    314 cal, 8 gm fat, 15 gm pro, 44 gm carb, 19 mg chol,
    381 mg sodium, 2 gm dietary fiber

Red and Green Pasta

Serve on Christmas Eve.

8 oz. dried penne pasta
3/4 c. sun-dried tomatoes
3/4 c. hot water
5 T. Pesto Sauce (see Index)
1 1/2 T. fresh grated Parmesan cheese

1. Cook pasta according to package directions, omitting salt and fat.
2. Soak tomatoes in hot water for 15 to 20 minutes until softened; drain and cut into small pieces.
3. Stir tomatoes and Pesto Sauce into cooked pasta.
4. Divide between 3 plates and top with Parmesan cheese.

Yield: 3 servings
Per Serving:
    397 cal, 8 gm fat, 16 gm pro, 62 gm carb, 6 mg chol,
    300 mg sodium, 4 gm dietary fiber

Penne Pasta with Feta Cheese and Sun-Dried Tomatoes

A pasta dish accented with feta cheese and sun-dried tomatoes; no need for sauce.

1/2 c. sun-dried tomatoes
1/2 c. hot water
6 oz. dried penne pasta
1 tsp. olive oil
2 tsp. minced garlic
2 T. chopped fresh basil
1 1/2 oz. feta cheese, crumbled

1. Soak tomatoes in hot water for 15 to 20 minutes, until soft enough to cut; drain and cut into small pieces.
2. Cook pasta according to package directions, omitting salt and fat.
3. While pasta is cooking, heat oil in a small saucepan. Add tomatoes, garlic and basil; sauté for a few minutes.
4. Add tomato mixture to pasta, along with feta cheese; stir to combine and serve.

Yield: 3 servings
Per Serving:
   277 cal, 6 gm fat, 11 gm pro, 46 gm carb, 13 mg chol,
   174 mg sodium, 1 gm dietary fiber

Chicken and Zucchini in Tomato Sauce

Serve family-style on a large platter.

3 1/2 tsp. olive oil, divided use
8 oz. sliced mushrooms
1/4 tsp. salt, divided use
3 c. sliced zucchini
3 T. flour
1/8 tsp. garlic powder
6 (4 oz.) boneless, skinless chicken breasts
1 c. chopped onion
1 (14 1/2 oz.) can chopped tomatoes, drained
2 T. balsamic vinegar
1 tsp. basil
1 tsp. oregano
8 oz. dried rigatoni pasta, cooked according to package directions, omitting salt & fat

1. Heat 1 teaspoon oil in a skillet and sauté mushrooms with 1/8 teaspoon salt for 6 to 8 minutes until browned. Remove and set aside.
2. In same skillet, add 1 teaspoon oil and sauté zucchini 4 to 5 minutes until tender and browned. Remove and set aside.
3. Stir together flour and garlic powder; coat chicken. In same skillet, heat remaining 1 1/2 teaspoons oil. Cook chicken for about 10 minutes until lightly browned on both sides and cooked through. Remove chicken and set aside.
4. Add onion to skillet and sauté until transparent.
5. Add drained tomatoes, vinegar, 1/8 teaspoon salt, basil, oregano, chicken and mushrooms; simmer for 5 minutes.
6. Add zucchini and cook for another 1 to 2 minutes.
7. Serve over pasta.

Yield: 6 servings
Per Serving:
354 cal, 7 gm fat, 34 gm pro, 36 gm carb, 72 mg chol, 333 mg sodium, 3 gm dietary fiber

Fettuccine with Chicken and Asparagus

A meal in itself.

4 (4 oz.) boneless, skinless chicken breasts
1 lb. fresh asparagus
1 tsp. margarine
4 green onions, chopped
1/4 tsp. salt
1/4 tsp. pepper
1/2 c. skim milk
1/2 c. half & half
Pinch of cayenne pepper
Pinch of nutmeg
2 oz. (1/2 c.) reduced-fat Swiss cheese, shredded
12 oz. dried fettuccine, cooked according to package directions, omitting salt & fat
3 T. Parmesan cheese

1. Cut chicken into bite-size strips and set aside.
2. Break off bottom 1/4 of asparagus and slice spears diagonally into 1-inch pieces. Steam for 2 minutes.
3. Heat margarine in a large skillet. Add green onions and chicken, stirring until the chicken is cooked through, about 2 to 3 minutes.
4. Season with salt and pepper; stir in asparagus. Sauté for 1 minute.
5. Stir in the milk, half and half, cayenne pepper and nutmeg. Add Swiss cheese and cook, stirring until cheese melts.
6. Combine pasta and sauce; divide among 6 plates. Top with Parmesan cheese.

Yield: 6 servings
Per Serving:
  425 cal, 9 gm fat, 33 gm pro, 49 gm carb, 63 mg chol,
  274 mg sodium, 5 gm dietary fiber

Baked Penne Pasta with Tomato Basil Sauce

A nice make-ahead dish.

1 stalk celery, chopped
3/4 c. chopped red onion
1 tsp. minced garlic
1/2 c. chopped fresh parsley
2 carrots, cut into matchstick strips
2 lb. tomatoes, chopped
2 tsp. olive oil
20 large fresh basil leaves, chopped, divided use
16 oz. dried penne pasta
6 oz. part-skim mozzarella cheese, cubed or shredded
2 tsp. oregano
3/4 tsp. salt
1/2 tsp. pepper
15 Greek olives, pitted & sliced
Nonstick vegetable cooking spray
1 tsp. parsley

1. In a large saucepan, combine celery, onion, garlic, parsley, carrots, tomatoes, olive oil and 1/4 basil. Simmer for 30 minutes, stirring every 5 minutes.
2. Cook penne pasta according to package directions, omitting salt and fat.
3. In a large bowl or the pot used for cooking the pasta, stir sauce, pasta, cheese, oregano, salt, pepper, olives and remaining basil together.
4. Spoon into a 9x13-inch baking dish that has been coated with cooking spray. Sprinkle with parsley.
5. Cover with foil and bake at 375°F. for 30 minutes.

Yield: 8 servings
Per Serving:
      334 cal, 8 gm fat, 15 gm pro, 48 gm carb, 11 mg chol,
      537 mg sodium, 4 gm dietary fiber

Mo's Great Lasagna

16 oz. dried lasagna noodles
1 lb. 90% lean ground beef
1 (26 oz.) jar spaghetti sauce
1 T. basil
2 tsp. oregano
1 tsp. Italian seasoning
1/2 tsp. tarragon
15 oz. part-skim ricotta cheese
6 oz. (1 1/2 c.) part-skim mozzarella cheese, shredded
1/4 c. Parmesan cheese

1. Cook noodles according to package directions, omitting salt and fat.
2. Brown ground beef in skillet; drain.
3. Wipe out skillet and return ground beef. Stir in spaghetti sauce and herbs.
4. To assemble, place 1 to 2 tablespoons of sauce mixture in bottom of a 9x13-inch baking dish. Layer with noodles, ricotta cheese, sauce mixture and mozzarella cheese, topping last layer of noodles with only sauce mixture.
5. Sprinkle with Parmesan cheese. Bake, covered, at 350°F. for 45 minutes, uncovering during last 10 minutes of baking. Remove from oven and let sit 10 minutes before serving.

Yield: 12 servings
Per Serving:
   329 cal, 10 gm fat, 22 gm pro, 35 gm carb, 43 mg chol,
   394 mg sodium, 2 gm dietary fiber

White Lasagna with Canadian Bacon

For artistic flair, serve this in a pool of tomato sauce.

15 (about 12 oz.) dried lasagna noodles
Nonstick vegetable cooking spray
16 oz. sliced mushrooms
1 large onion, chopped
2 tsp. minced garlic
1 (14 oz.) can artichoke hearts, drained & chopped
3 c. nonfat cottage cheese
1 c. skim milk
2 oz. blue cheese, crumbled
6 oz. Canadian bacon, chopped
4 c. fresh spinach (optional)
3/4 c. Parmesan cheese

1. Cook noodles according to package directions, omitting salt and fat.
2. Coat a large skillet with cooking spray and sauté mushrooms for 5 minutes. Add onions and garlic. Continue to sauté until vegetables are soft, about 5 more minutes. Drain liquid and return vegetables to skillet.
3. Stir in artichoke hearts.
4. Place cottage cheese in a food processor and process until cheese is smooth. Transfer it to a mixing bowl and stir in milk, blue cheese and Canadian bacon.
5. If including spinach, steam for 2 to 3 minutes until it is just wilted.
6. Spoon 1/5 vegetable mixture over the bottom of a 9x13-inch baking dish. Cover with noodles and spread 1/5 of cheese mixture over the top. Layer 1 more time in the same order. Layer spinach on top and continue layering as before, ending with cheese mixture.

Continued on following page.

Continued from preceding page.

7.   Sprinkle with Parmesan cheese.
8.   Bake at 350°F. for 40 minutes or until top is browned. Remove from oven and allow to sit for 10 minutes before serving*.

*After you cut the first piece, drain any extra liquid that might have accumulated.

Yield: 12 servings
Per Serving:
    232 cal, 5 gm fat, 19 gm pro, 29 gm carb, 19 mg chol,
    658 mg sodium, 2 gm dietary fiber

Lasagna with Grilled Chicken and Pesto

This nontraditional lasagna makes use of our famous Pesto Sauce.

12 (~9 1/2 oz.) dried lasagna noodles
16 oz. low-fat cottage cheese
1/2 c. chicken broth
1 c. Pesto Sauce (see Index)
4 (4 oz.) boneless, skinless chicken breasts, grilled & thinly sliced
1 onion, cut into rings & grilled
7 oz. (1 3/4 c.) part-skim mozzarella cheese, shredded
2 T. fresh grated Parmesan cheese

1. Cook noodles according to package directions, omitting salt and fat.
2. Place cottage cheese in food processor and process until smooth.
3. Stir chicken broth and Pesto Sauce together.
4. To assemble, spread 1 to 2 tablespoons pesto mixture in the bottom of a 9x13-inch baking dish. Layer with noodles, cottage cheese, pesto mixture, chicken, onions and mozzarella cheese, topping last layer of noodles with only pesto mixture and mozzarella cheese.
5. Sprinkle with Parmesan cheese and bake at 350°F. for 40 minutes or until top is browned. Remove from oven and let sit 10 minutes before serving.

Yield: 12 servings
Per Serving:
    269 cal, 9 gm fat, 25 gm pro, 20 gm carb, 38 mg chol,
    576 mg sodium, 1 gm dietary fiber

With the availability of many reduced-fat cheeses and pre-made crusts, pizza can be a quick and low-fat alternative to doorstep delivery.

Canadian Bacon Pizza

1/2 c. spaghetti sauce
1 (14 oz.) pizza crust*
4 oz. (1 c.) part-skim mozzarella cheese, shredded
1 1/2 oz. Canadian bacon, chopped
1 Roma or plum tomato, sliced
1/2 tsp. oregano
1/2 tsp. basil

*We use Kabuli pizza crust which is made without fat and available in the grocery store.

1. Spread sauce over pizza crust and top with cheese, Canadian bacon, tomato slices, oregano and basil.
2. Bake at 400°F. for 10 minutes. Cut into 8 pieces.

Yield: 4 servings
Per Serving (2 pieces):
    381 cal, 7 gm fat, 19 gm pro, 57 gm carb, 21 mg chol,
    772 mg sodium, 5 gm dietary fiber

Sun-Dried Tomato and Feta Cheese Pizza

1/3 c. sun-dried tomatoes
1/3 c. hot water
3/4 c. spaghetti sauce
1 (14 oz.) pizza crust*
3 oz. (3/4 c.) part-skim mozzarella cheese, shredded
1 1/2 oz. feta cheese, crumbled
1/2 tsp. oregano
1/2 tsp. basil

*We use Kabuli pizza crust which is made without fat and available in the grocery store.

1. Soak tomatoes in hot water for 15 to 20 minutes; drain and cut into small pieces.
2. Spread sauce over pizza crust and top with mozzarella cheese, tomatoes, feta cheese, oregano and basil.
3. Bake at 400°F. for 10 minutes. Cut into 8 pieces.

Yield: 4 servings
Per Serving (2 pieces):
    386 cal, 7 gm fat, 17 gm pro, 59 gm carb, 21 mg chol,
    764 mg sodium, 5 gm dietary fiber

Barbecued Chicken Pizza

Two old favorites, barbecue and pizza, make a double-hitter.

4 T. barbecue sauce, divided use
2 (4 oz.) boneless, skinless chicken breasts
1 (14 oz.) pizza crust*
4 oz. (1 c.) part-skim mozzarella cheese, shredded
1/4 c. chopped green onions
1/4 c. chopped cilantro

*We use Kabuli pizza crust which is made without fat and available in the grocery store.

1. Spread 1 tablespoon barbecue sauce over the 2 chicken breasts and bake at 350°F. for 20 to 30 minutes, until cooked through. Cut into bite-size strips.
2. Spread remaining 3 tablespoons barbecue sauce over pizza crust and top with cheese, chicken, green onions and cilantro.
3. Bake at 400°F. for 10 minutes. Cut into 8 pieces.

Yield: 4 servings
Per Serving (2 pieces):
   428 cal, 7 gm fat, 30 gm pro, 56 gm carb, 51 mg chol,
   673 mg sodium, 5 gm dietary fiber

Pesto and Cheddar Pizza

For adventurous types, add mushrooms and artichoke hearts.

1 (14 oz.) pizza crust*
6 T. Pesto Sauce (see Index)
2 1/2 oz. (10 T.) reduced-fat Cheddar cheese, shredded

*We use Kabuli pizza crust which is made without fat and available in the grocery store.

1. Spread Pesto Sauce over pizza crust and top with Cheddar cheese.
2. Bake at 400°F. for 10 minutes. Cut into 8 pieces.

Yield: 4 servings
Per Serving (2 pieces):
    368 cal, 8 gm fat, 16 gm pro, 54 gm carb, 13 mg chol,
    638 mg sodium, 4 gm dietary fiber

Mexican Pizza

*Easiest way to receive culinary accolades from all ages.
Also, this pizza is a great source of fiber.*

1 red bell pepper, cut into strips
1 green bell pepper, cut into strips
1 c. sliced mushrooms
1 1/4 c. sliced purple onions, divided use
1/2 c. picante sauce
Nonstick vegetable cooking spray
1 tsp. minced garlic
1 c. cooked or canned black beans, drained & rinsed of bean liquid
1 (4 oz.) can chopped green chilies
1 (14 oz.) pizza crust*
1 1/4 oz. (5 T.) reduced-fat Monterey Jack cheese, shredded
1 1/4 oz. (5 T.) reduced-fat Cheddar cheese, shredded
2 to 4 fresh jalapeños, seeded & chopped
1 oz. feta cheese, crumbled
1/2 c. chopped cilantro

*We use Kabuli pizza crust which is made without fat and available
in the grocery store.

1. Stir peppers, mushrooms, 1 cup onions and picante sauce
    together. Allow to marinate for 2 to 3 hours; drain liquid.
2. In a skillet that has been coated with cooking spray, sauté garlic
    and 1/4 cup onion until onion is transparent. Add black beans
    and green chilies; cook for 5 minutes, mashing beans while
    cooking. If mixture becomes dry, add 1 tablespoon water.
3. Spread black bean mixture over crust and top with marinated
    vegetables.
4. Sprinkle with Monterey Jack and Cheddar cheese, jalapeños,
    then feta cheese.
5. Bake at 400°F. for 10 minutes, adding cilantro to top, after first
    5 minutes.

Yield: 4 servings
Per Serving (2 pieces):
    444 cal, 6 gm fat, 20 gm pro, 67 gm carb, 16 mg chol,
    781 mg sodium, 11 gm dietary fiber

Risotto with Sun-Dried Tomatoes and Mozzarella Cheese

Mellow in color, vibrant in taste.

1/2 c. sun-dried tomatoes
1/2 c. hot water
6 c. low-sodium chicken broth, defatted*
1/3 c. white wine
2 tsp. olive oil
1/3 c. onion
1 1/2 tsp. minced garlic
1 1/2 c. uncooked arborio rice
2 oz. (1/2 c.) part-skim mozzarella cheese, shredded
1/2 tsp. salt
4 T. fresh grated Parmesan cheese

*If using canned or homemade chicken broth, defat by placing in refrigerator. When cold, skim fat off the top.

1. Soak tomatoes in hot water for 15 to 20 minutes. Drain and cut into small pieces.
2. Bring chicken broth to a boil. Add wine and reduce heat so the liquid remains simmering.
3. In a large saucepan, heat oil. Add onion and garlic; sauté until onion is slightly transparent.
4. Add rice and sauté for 2 to 3 minutes.
5. Start adding chicken broth, 1/2 cup at a time, each time stirring until liquid is absorbed. Continue cooking until all broth has been added, adding tomatoes after the first 10 minutes of cooking. Total cooking time should be about 20 minutes.
6. Stir in mozzarella cheese and salt.
7. Ladle into large bowls and sprinkle with Parmesan cheese.

Yield: 4 servings
Per Serving:
    392 cal, 7 gm fat, 13 gm pro, 63 gm carb, 13 mg chol,
    548 mg sodium, 1 gm dietary fiber

Seafood Risotto

The shrimp is added at the end to avoid overcooking.

3 1/2 tsp. olive oil, divided use
1 c. chopped onion
1 tsp. minced garlic
4 oz. sliced mushrooms
2 T. fresh parsley or 1/2 T. dried parsley
1/4 c. fresh basil or 1 T. dried basil
1 tsp. fresh tarragon or 1/4 tsp. dried tarragon
Dash of cayenne pepper
1/4 tsp. pepper
2 1/2 c. chopped Roma or plum tomatoes
3/4 lb. medium (36 to 40 count) shrimp, peeled & deveined
6 c. low-sodium chicken broth, defatted*
1 c. white wine
2 T. chopped shallots
2 c. uncooked arborio rice
1 1/2 oz. (6 T.) fresh grated Parmesan cheese
3/4 tsp. salt

*If using canned or homemade chicken broth, defat by placing in refrigerator. When cold, skim fat off the top.

1. Heat 1 1/2 teaspoons oil in a saucepan and sauté onion until transparent. Add garlic and mushrooms; cook over low heat for 5 minutes.
2. Add herbs, pepper and tomatoes; cook 15 minutes. Add shrimp and cook for 5 more minutes; set aside.
3. Bring chicken broth to a boil. Add wine and reduce heat so that liquid remains simmering.
4. Heat remaining 2 teaspoons oil in a large saucepan and sauté shallots for 2 to 3 minutes.
5. Add rice and sauté for 2 to 3 minutes.

Continued on following page.

126

Continued from preceding page.

6. Start adding chicken broth, 1/2 cup at a time, each time stirring
    until liquid is absorbed. Continue cooking until all broth has
    been added. Total cooking time should be about 20 minutes.
7. Reheat sauce and stir into risotto. Ladle into bowls and sprinkle
    with cheese.

Yield: 6 servings
Per Serving (1 1/4 cups):
    373 cal, 6 gm fat, 15 gm pro, 56 gm carb, 61 mg chol,
    583 mg sodium, 2 gm dietary fiber

Risotto with Blue Cheese

Truly, a comfort food.

7 c. low-sodium chicken broth, defatted*
1 tsp. olive oil
2 c. uncooked arborio rice
1/4 c. skim milk
3 oz. blue cheese
1 tsp. salt
1/2 tsp. pepper

*If using canned or homemade chicken broth, defat by placing in refrigerator. When cold, skim fat off the top.

1. Bring broth to a boil and then lower heat to keep it simmering.
2. In a large saucepan, heat oil. Stir in rice and sauté for 2 to 3 minutes.
3. Start adding the simmering broth, 1/2 cup at a time, each time stirring until liquid is absorbed. Continue cooking until all broth has been added. Total cooking time should be about 20 minutes.
4. Stir in milk, cheese, salt and pepper; serve hot.

Yield: 5 servings
Per Serving (1 cup):
    351 cal, 6 gm fat, 16 gm pro, 58 gm carb, 13 mg chol,
    683 mg sodium, 1 gm dietary fiber

Primavera Sauce

Make a trip to the Farmers Market for this one.

2 small (1 1/2 lb.) eggplants, sliced 1/4-inch thick
1 T. plus 2 tsp. salt, divided use
1 T. olive oil
1 large onion, chopped
2 tsp. minced garlic
4 1/2 lb. Roma or plum tomatoes, chopped
8 oz. sliced mushrooms
5 carrots, peeled & sliced
1 1/2 c. red wine
2/3 c. fresh basil or 2 1/2 T. dried basil
1 T. parsley
1 T. oregano
1 tsp. rosemary
1/8 tsp. ground cloves
1/4 tsp. cayenne pepper
3/4 tsp. pepper

1. Salt both sides of eggplant slices with 1 tablespoon salt. Allow the slices to drain in a colander for 45 minutes. Rinse well with water. Shake off excess water and chop slices into 1-inch pieces.
2. Heat oil in a large stockpot. Add onion and garlic. Sauté until onion is transparent. Add all remaining ingredients and simmer for 1 1/2 to 2 hours.
3. Serve over tri-color spiral (rotini) pasta.

Yield: 13 servings
Per Serving (1 cup sauce):
   100 cal, 2 gm fat, 3 gm pro, 16 gm carb, 0 mg chol,
   354 mg sodium, 5 gm dietary fiber

Pesto Sauce

From our first cookbook. Freeze in one tablespoon increments in ice trays. When frozen, place cubes in a plastic bag. Use in recipes such as Pesto and Cheddar Pizza, Red and Green Pasta, and Pesto-Crusted Potato Wedges.

4 c. fresh basil
1 1/2 T. olive oil
2 T. chicken broth
2 garlic cloves
2 T. parsley
1/2 tsp. salt
1/8 tsp. pepper
1/4 c. walnuts or pine nuts
1/2 c. Parmesan cheese

1. Place basil in bowl of food processor.
2. Pour remaining ingredients on top and process until all ingredients are combined.
3. Toss 1 tablespoon of sauce with 1 cup of your favorite pasta.

Yield: 16 servings
Per Serving (1 tablespoon):
    39 cal, 3 gm fat, 2 gm pro, 1 gm carb, 2 mg chol,
    123 mg sodium, 0 gm dietary fiber

Notes & Recipes

Breakfast and Brunch

Blueberry Cornmeal Pancakes

French Toast with Fresh Strawberries

Cinnamon French Toast

Pecan French Toast

Apricot Raisin Granola

Chicken and Poblano Quiche

Spinach Quiche

Hash Brown Casserole

Blueberry Cornmeal Pancakes

Bursting with blueberries!

2/3 c. flour
1/3 c. cornmeal
2 T. sugar
3/4 tsp. baking powder
1/4 tsp. baking soda
1/4 tsp. salt
1 c. buttermilk
4 egg whites, divided use
1 1/2 tsp. margarine, melted
1 c. fresh blueberries

1. Stir together flour, cornmeal, sugar, baking powder, baking soda and salt.
2. In a separate bowl, combine buttermilk, 2 egg whites and margarine.
3. Stir milk mixture into flour mixture just until flour is moistened.
4. Beat remaining 2 egg whites until stiff. Fold into pancake mixture.
5. Pour approximately 1/4 cup of batter onto a hot griddle. Sprinkle with a few blueberries when edges start to dry. Cook until bubbles form and break.
6. Flip and cook until browned.

Yield: 3 servings
Per Serving (3 pancakes):
    289 cal, 3 gm fat, 12 gm pro, 51 gm carb, 3 mg chol,
    558 mg sodium, 2 gm dietary fiber

The incredible edible egg substitutes make low-cholesterol French Toast.

French Toast with Fresh Strawberries

3/4 c. egg substitute or 6 egg whites
1 tsp. sugar
1 tsp. vanilla extract
4 slices French bread
Nonstick vegetable cooking spray
1 c. sliced fresh strawberries
2 T. powdered sugar

1. Stir egg substitute or egg whites, sugar and vanilla together in a dish large enough to lay 1 slice of bread flat.
2. Dip each slice of bread in egg mixture, coating both sides.
3. Place in a skillet that has been coated with cooking spray and cook until browned on both sides.
4. Place on 2 plates and top with strawberries. Sift powdered sugar over the top and serve.

Yield: 2 servings
Per Serving (2 slices):
246 cal, 2 gm fat, 13 gm pro, 45 gm carb, 0 mg chol, 411 mg sodium, 3 gm dietary fiber.

Cinnamon French Toast

1/2 c. egg substitute or 4 egg whites
1/3 c. skim milk
1 tsp. cinnamon
4 slices reduced-calorie bread (40 calories per slice)
Nonstick vegetable cooking spray

1. Stir egg substitute or egg whites, skim milk and cinnamon together in a dish large enough to lay 1 slice of bread flat.
2. Dip each slice of bread in egg mixture, coating both sides.
3. Place in a skillet that has been coated with cooking spray, and brown on both sides.

Yield: 2 servings
Per Serving (2 slices):
    136 cal, 2 gm fat, 9 gm pro, 23 gm carb, 1 mg chol,
    293 mg sodium, 1 gm dietary fiber

Pecan French Toast

1 c. egg substitute or 8 egg whites
2/3 c. orange juice
1/3 c. skim milk
1/4 c. sugar
1/2 tsp. nutmeg
1/2 tsp. vanilla extract
8 slices reduced-calorie bread (40 calories per slice)
Nonstick vegetable cooking spray
3 T. chopped pecans
1 tsp. grated orange peel

1. Whisk egg substitute or egg whites, juice, milk, sugar, nutmeg and vanilla together.
2. Place bread in a pan just large enough to lay bread in a single layer. Pour egg mixture over bread.
3. Cover and refrigerate overnight, turning once.
4. Transfer bread to a jelly-roll pan that has been coated with cooking spray.
5. Sprinkle bread with pecans and orange peel.
6. Bake at 400°F. for 20 to 25 minutes, until golden brown.

Yield: 4 servings
Per Serving (2 slices):
  219 cal, 2 gm fat, 10 gm pro, 40 gm carb, 0 mg chol,
  353 mg sodium, 5 gm dietary fiber

Apricot Raisin Granola

Normally a high-fat cereal, enjoy this low-fat granola.

3 c. rolled oats
1/3 c. brown sugar, firmly packed
1/3 c. honey
1/4 c. orange juice
2 T. vanilla extract
3/4 tsp. salt
1 c. raisins
1 c. chopped dried apricots
Nonstick vegetable cooking spray

1. Stir all ingredients, except raisins and apricots together.
2. Spoon into a 9x13-inch baking dish that has been coated with cooking spray.
3. Bake at 350°F. for 40 minutes, adding raisins and apricots after first 20 minutes. Stir mixture every 10 minutes.
4. Allow to cool and store in airtight container.

Yield: 10 servings
Per Serving (1/2 cup):
    242 cal, 2 gm fat, 5 gm pro, 53 gm carb, 0 mg chol,
    167 mg sodium, 4 gm dietary fiber

A typical piece of quiche can add forty-two grams of fat to your daily allotment of fat. These quiche recipes will not tip the fat scale.

Chicken and Poblano Quiche

1 1/4 c. flour
1/4 tsp. salt
1 1/2 T. sugar
4 T. margarine
2 to 4 T. ice-cold water
1/2 c. sun-dried tomatoes
1/2 c. hot water
3/4 c. egg substitute
1 c. evaporated skim milk
1 T. chopped green onions
1/2 tsp. salt
1 tsp. pepper
1/2 c. chopped poblano peppers
6 oz. cooked, skinless chicken breasts, shredded
3 oz. (3/4 c.) reduced-fat Monterey Jack cheese, shredded

1. Add flour, salt, sugar and margarine to a food processor. Pulse for 30 seconds until mixture resembles cornmeal. Add ice-cold water, 1 tablespoon at a time, until the mixture just holds together.
2. Form the dough into a disk and place between 2 large pieces of wax paper. Chill in the refrigerator for 1 hour.
3. Roll pie dough into a circle 2 inches larger than pie pan. Line the pan with the dough and crimp the edges.
4. Soak tomatoes in hot water for 15 to 20 minutes until soft; drain and cut into small pieces.
5. Combine egg substitute, evaporated milk, green onions, salt and pepper. Stir in tomatoes, poblano peppers, chicken and cheese.
6. Pour egg mixture into crust and bake at 350°F. for 45 minutes. Let cool a few minutes and serve warm.

Yield: 8 servings
Per Serving:
    243 cal, 9 gm fat, 16 gm pro, 25 gm carb, 25 mg chol,
    413 mg sodium, 1 gm dietary fiber

Spinach Quiche

1 1/4 c. flour
3/4 tsp. plus 1/8 tsp. salt, divided use
1 1/2 T. sugar
4 T. margarine
2 to 4 T. ice-cold water
8 oz. sliced mushrooms
Nonstick vegetable cooking spray
1 (10 oz.) package frozen, chopped spinach
3/4 c. egg substitute
1 c. evaporated skim milk
1 T. chopped green onions
1 tsp. pepper
Dash of nutmeg
4 oz. (1 c.) reduced-fat Swiss cheese, shredded

1. Add flour, 1/4 teaspoon salt, sugar and margarine to a food processor. Pulse for 30 seconds, until mixture resembles cornmeal. Add ice-cold water, 1 tablespoon at a time, until the mixture just holds together.
2. Form the dough into a disk and place between 2 large pieces of wax paper. Chill in the refrigerator for 1 hour.
3. Roll pie dough into a circle 2 inches larger than pie pan. Line the pan with the dough and crimp the edges.
4. Add mushrooms and 1/8 teaspoon salt to a skillet that has been coated with cooking spray; sauté until browned, about 6 to 8 minutes.
5. Defrost spinach and squeeze all water from it.
6. Combine egg substitute, evaporated milk, green onions, 1/2 teaspoon salt, pepper and nutmeg. Stir in mushrooms, spinach and cheese.
7. Pour egg mixture into crust and bake at 350°F. for 45 minutes. Let cool a few minutes and serve warm.

Yield: 8 servings
Per Serving:
    219 cal, 9 gm fat, 11 gm pro, 23 gm carb, 9 mg chol,
    467 mg sodium, 2 gm dietary fiber

Hash Brown Casserole

Start your day off right with a hearty breakfast.

2 tsp. canola oil
1 (2 lb.) bag frozen hash browns
1 onion, chopped
1 green bell pepper, chopped
Nonstick vegetable cooking spray
4 oz. Canadian bacon, chopped
2 1/2 c. egg substitute
1/4 tsp. salt
1/2 tsp. pepper
4 oz. (1 c.) reduced-fat Cheddar cheese, shredded

1. Heat oil in a large skillet. Add hash browns, onions and green peppers. Cook until potatoes begin to brown.
2. Spread potato mixture into a 9x13-inch baking dish that has been coated with cooking spray. Add Canadian bacon, egg substitute, salt and pepper; stir to coat all ingredients with egg.
3. Sprinkle cheese on top.
4. Cover with foil and refrigerate overnight.
5. Bake, covered, for 30 to 40 minutes at 375°F. Remove foil and bake for 5 more minutes, or until egg mixture is set.

Yield: 8 servings
Per Serving:
198 cal, 5 gm fat, 14 gm pro, 22 gm carb, 15 mg chol, 550 mg sodium, 4 gm dietary fiber

Breads and Muffins

Blueberry Lemon Bread
Banana Chocolate Chip Bread
Banana Apricot Muffins
Cranberry Orange Muffins
Oatmeal Butterscotch Muffins
Carrot Cake Muffins
Strawberry Cornmeal Muffins
Blue Corn Muffins
Jalapeño Cornbread
Cherry and Orange Scones
Irish Soda Bread Scones
Cheese and Scallion Scones

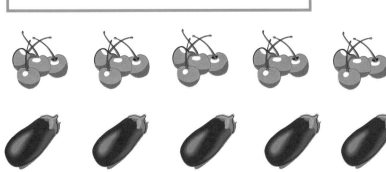

Blueberry Lemon Bread

Lemon apeel!

3 T. margarine, softened
1 c. sugar
4 egg whites or 1/2 c. egg substitute
1 1/2 c. flour
1 T. baking powder
1 tsp. salt
1/2 c. skim milk
1 c. fresh blueberries
1 T. grated lemon peel
1 tsp. lemon juice
Nonstick vegetable cooking spray

1. With a mixer, cream margarine and sugar together.
2. Add egg whites or egg substitute; mix well.
3. In a separate bowl, combine flour, baking powder and salt.
4. Stir flour mixture into creamed mixture a little at a time, alternating with milk. Stir just until flour is moistened.
5. Fold in blueberries, lemon peel and juice.
6. Pour batter into a loaf pan, that has been coated with cooking spray.
7. Bake at 350°F. for 50 to 60 minutes, until toothpick inserted in center comes out clean.

Yield: 12 servings
Per Serving:
155 cal, 3 gm fat, 3 gm pro, 30 gm carb, 0 mg chol,
332 mg sodium, 1 gm dietary fiber

Banana Chocolate Chip Bread

Serve it warm with sliced bananas.

2 c. flour
1/2 c. brown sugar, firmly packed
2 tsp. baking powder
1/4 tsp. salt
4 egg whites or 1/2 c. egg substitute
2 bananas, mashed
1/3 c. reduced-calorie maple syrup
1 T. canola oil
1/4 c. skim milk
1/3 c. chocolate chips
Nonstick vegetable cooking spray

1. In a large bowl, combine flour, sugar, baking powder and salt.
2. In a small bowl, beat egg whites; add bananas, syrup, oil and milk. Add to flour mixture, stirring just until moistened.
3. Fold in chocolate chips.
4. Pour batter into a loaf pan, that has been coated with cooking spray.
5. Bake at 350°F. for 60 to 65 minutes, until toothpick inserted in center comes out clean.
6. Cool for 10 minutes before removing from pan.

Yield: 16 servings
Per Serving:
   139 cal, 2 gm fat, 3 gm pro, 27 gm carb, 0 mg chol,
   125 mg sodium, 1 gm dietary fiber

Banana Apricot Muffins

Not your ordinary banana bread, you'll enjoy the change!

2 T. margarine
1/3 c. brown sugar, firmly packed
1/3 c. sugar
4 egg whites or 1/2 c. egg substitute
2 c. flour
1/2 tsp. salt
1/2 tsp. baking soda
3 bananas, mashed
1/4 c. chopped walnuts
3/4 c. chopped dried apricots
Nonstick vegetable cooking spray

1. With a mixer, cream margarine and sugars together.
2. Add egg whites or egg substitute; mix well.
3. In a separate bowl, combine flour, salt and baking soda.
4. Stir flour mixture into creamed mixture a little at a time, alternating with the mashed bananas. Stir just until flour is moistened.
5. Fold in walnuts and apricots.
6. Spoon batter into muffin tins, that have been coated with cooking spray.
7. Bake at 350°F. for 18 to 20 minutes, until lightly browned on top.

Yield: 12 muffins
Per Serving (1 muffin):
    196 cal, 4 gm fat, 4 gm pro, 38 gm carb, 0 mg chol,
    162 mg sodium, 2 gm dietary fiber.

Cranberry Orange Muffins

No fat in these muffins!

2 c. flour
3/4 c. sugar
1/2 tsp. baking soda
1 1/2 tsp. baking powder
1/2 tsp. salt
1 c. orange juice
2 egg whites or 1/4 c. egg substitute
1 1/4 c. chopped fresh cranberries
Nonstick vegetable cooking spray

1. Combine flour, sugar, baking soda, baking powder and salt.
2. Stir in orange juice, and egg whites or egg substitute, until flour is just moistened.
3. Fold in cranberries.
4. Spoon batter into muffin tins, that have been coated with cooking spray.
5. Bake at 350°F. for 22 to 28 minutes, until lightly browned on top.

Yield: 12 muffins
Per Serving (1 muffin):
132 cal, 0 gm fat, 3 gm pro, 31 gm carb, 0 mg chol,
183 mg sodium, 1 gm dietary fiber

Oatmeal Butterscotch Muffins

3 c. rolled oats
1 pt. buttermilk
1 c. brown sugar, firmly packed
1/4 c. margarine, melted
6 egg whites or 3/4 c. egg substitute
1 c. flour
1/2 c. wholewheat flour
2 tsp. baking powder
1/2 tsp. salt
3/4 tsp. baking soda
1/2 c. butterscotch chips
Nonstick vegetable cooking spray

1. In a large bowl, combine oats and buttermilk; mix well. Crumble brown sugar over top and let stand for 1 hour in refrigerator.
2. Add margarine, and egg whites or egg substitute, to oatmeal mixture and mix well.
3. Combine flours, baking powder, salt and baking soda.
4. Stir flour mixture into oatmeal mixture, just until flour is moistened.
5. Fold in butterscotch chips.
6. Spoon batter into muffin tins, that have been coated with cooking spray.
7. Bake at 400°F. for 15 to 20 minutes, until lightly browned on top.

Yield: 24 muffins
Per Serving (1 muffin):
    147 cal, 4 gm fat, 4 gm pro, 24 gm carb, 1 mg chol,
    166 mg sodium, 1 gm dietary fiber

Carrot Cake Muffins

The yummy taste of carrot cake in a muffin.

2 T. margarine
3/4 c. sugar
4 egg whites or 1/2 c. egg substitute
1 c. flour
1/2 c. wholewheat flour
1/2 tsp. salt
1 1/2 tsp. baking powder
1 tsp. cinnamon
1 tsp. nutmeg
1/2 c. skim milk
1 1/4 c. grated carrots
2 T. chopped pecans
1/2 c. golden raisins
Nonstick vegetable cooking spray

1. With a mixer, cream margarine and sugar together.
2. Add egg whites or egg substitute and mix well.
3. In a separate bowl, combine flours, salt, baking powder, cinnamon and nutmeg.
4. Stir flour mixture into creamed mixture a little at a time, alternating with milk. Stir just until flour is moistened.
5. Fold in carrots, pecans and raisins.
6. Spoon batter into muffin tins, that have been coated with cooking spray.
7. Bake at 350°F. for 22 to 25 minutes, until lightly browned on top.

Yield: 12 muffins
Per Serving (1 muffin):
    166 cal, 3 gm fat, 4 gm pro, 31 gm carb, 0 mg chol,
    189 mg sodium, 2 gm dietary fiber

Strawberry Cornmeal Muffins

Serve alongside a fruit salad, or as a dessert topped with additional strawberries and Cool Whip Lite.

2 T. margarine, softened
1 1/4 c. powdered sugar
4 egg whites or 1/2 c. egg substitute
1 1/4 c. flour
1 tsp. baking powder
1/8 tsp. salt
1/2 c. skim milk
1/2 c. cornmeal
1 c. sliced fresh strawberries
Nonstick vegetable cooking spray

1. With a mixer, cream margarine. Gradually beat in powdered sugar, scraping bowl as needed, until mixture is fluffy. Beat in egg whites or egg substitute.
2. In a separate bowl, combine flour, baking powder and salt.
3. Stir flour mixture into creamed mixture a little at a time, alternating with milk; blend thoroughly.
4. Stir in cornmeal and strawberries.
5. Spoon batter into muffin tins, that have been coated with cooking spray.
6. Bake at 350°F. for 30 minutes, or until lightly browned on top.

Yield: 12 muffins
Per Serving (1 muffin):
    147 cal, 2 gm fat, 3 gm pro, 28 gm carb, 0 mg chol,
    100 mg sodium, 1 gm dietary fiber

Blue Corn Muffins

Serve with Sagamity or Black Bean Chili. Blue corn-meal is available at specially grocery stores. You can also use yellow cornmeal.

1 c. blue cornmeal
1 1/4 c. flour
1/2 c. sugar
1 1/2 tsp. baking powder
1/2 tsp. cinnamon
1/8 tsp. ground cloves
1/8 tsp. salt
2 egg whites or 1/4 c. egg substitute
1 c. skim milk
2 T. margarine, melted
2 T. pine nuts
Nonstick vegetable cooking spray

1. In a large bowl, stir together cornmeal, flour, sugar, baking powder, cinnamon, cloves and salt.
2. Stir in egg whites or egg substitute, milk and margarine.
3. Fold in pine nuts.
4. Spoon batter into muffin tins, that have been coated with cooking spray.
5. Bake at 400°F. for 20 to 25 minutes, until lightly browned on top.

Yield: 12 muffins
Per Serving (1 muffin):
   158 cal, 3 gm fat, 4 gm pro, 28 gm carb, 0 mg chol,
   110 mg sodium, 1 gm dietary fiber

Jalapeño Cornbread

A truly Southern bread once flavored with bacon fat, this version has the same flair minus the fat.

1/2 c. skim milk
4 egg whites or 1/2 c. egg substitute
3 oz. (3/4 c.) reduced-fat Cheddar cheese, shredded
1 c. cream-style canned corn
1/4 c. picante sauce
1 c. cornmeal
1/2 c. flour
1 T. baking powder
Nonstick vegetable cooking spray

1. In a large bowl, combine milk, egg whites or egg substitute, cheese, corn and picante sauce.
2. In a separate bowl, combine cornmeal, flour and baking powder.
3. Stir flour mixture into milk mixture, blending well.
4. Pour batter into a 9x9-inch pan, that has been coated with cooking spray.
5. Bake at 375°F. for 20 minutes.

Yield: 16 servings
Per Serving:
    80 cal, 1 gm fat, 4 gm pro, 14 gm carb, 3 mg chol,
    185 mg sodium, 1 gm dietary fiber

Cherry and Orange Scones

Serve with English tea for a low-fat tea time treat.

2 c. flour
1/4 c. sugar
2 tsp. baking powder
1/2 tsp. salt
3 T. margarine
4 egg whites or 1/2 c. egg substitute
3 T. orange juice
1 tsp. vanilla extract
1/2 tsp. orange peel
1/3 c. dried cherries
Nonstick vegetable cooking spray

1. Place flour, sugar, baking powder, salt and margarine in food processor and process until mixture resembles coarse meal. Or place ingredients in a bowl and cut in margarine, using a pastry blender.
2. In a separate bowl, stir together egg whites or egg substitute, orange juice, vanilla and orange peel.
3. Stir flour mixture into egg mixture, just until flour is moistened.
4. Fold in cherries.
5. On a baking sheet, that has been coated with cooking spray, spread dough into a 9-inch circle. With a serrated knife, cut circle into 10 wedges, cutting only halfway through dough.
6. Bake at 375°F. for 15 to 20 minutes, until lightly browned on top.

Yield: 10 servings
Per Serving (1 scone):
   158 cal, 4 gm fat, 4 gm pro, 27 gm carb, 0 mg chol,
   242 mg sodium, 0 gm dietary fiber

Irish Soda Bread Scones

2 c. flour
3 T. brown sugar, firmly packed
1 1/2 tsp. baking powder
1/2 tsp. baking soda
1/2 tsp. caraway seed
1/4 tsp. salt
2 1/2 T. margarine
2 egg whites or 1/4 c. egg substitute
1/2 c. buttermilk
1/3 c. currants
2 T. chopped walnuts
Nonstick vegetable cooking spray

1. Place flour, sugar, baking powder, baking soda, caraway seed, salt and margarine in food processor and process until mixture resembles coarse meal. Or place ingredients in a bowl and cut in margarine, using a pastry blender.
2. In a separate bowl, stir together egg whites or egg substitute and buttermilk.
3. Stir flour mixture into egg mixture, just until flour is moistened.
4. Fold in currants.
5. On a baking sheet, that has been coated with cooking spray, spread dough into a 9-inch circle. Sprinkle with nuts. With a serrated knife, cut circle into 10 wedges, cutting only halfway through dough.
6. Bake at 375°F. for 15 to 20 minutes, until lightly browned on top.

Yield: 10 servings
Per Serving (1 scone):
    164 cal, 4 gm fat, 4 gm pro, 27 gm carb, 0 mg chol,
    230 mg sodium, 1 gm dietary fiber

Cheese and Scallion Scones

Serve as an appetizer or with tomato soup.

2 c. flour
2 tsp. baking powder
1/4 tsp. salt
1/8 tsp. cayenne pepper
2 oz. (1/2 c.) part-skim mozzarella cheese, shredded
1 1/2 T. Parmesan cheese
2 1/2 T. margarine
4 egg whites or 1/2 c. egg substitute
1/3 c. skim milk
2 T. chopped scallions (green onions)
1 tsp. basil
Nonstick vegetable cooking spray
1/2 tsp. oregano

1. Place flour, baking powder, salt, pepper, cheeses and margarine in food processor and process until mixture resembles coarse meal. Or place ingredients in a bowl and cut in margarine, using a pastry blender.
2. In a separate bowl, stir together egg whites or egg substitute, skim milk, scallions and basil.
3. Stir flour mixture into egg mixture, just until flour is moistened.
4. On a baking sheet, that has been coated with cooking spray, spread dough into a 9-inch circle. With a serrated knife, cut circle into 10 wedges, cutting only halfway through dough. Sprinkle with oregano.
5. Bake at 375°F. for 15 to 18 minutes, until lightly browned on top.

Yield: 10 servings
Per Serving (1 scone):
    147 cal, 4 gm fat, 6 gm pro, 20 gm carb, 4 mg chol,
    230 mg sodium, 0 gm dietary fiber

Desserts

A Recommendation for Desserts
Dutch Apple Crumble
Pear Raspberry Crumble
Blueberry and Cream Pie
Lemon Meringue Pie
Key Lime Pie
French Strawberry Pie
Very Berry Pie
Raspberry Pie
Brownie Pie
Chocolate Chip and Peppermint Brownie
Pie
Strawberry, Blueberry and Raspberry
Cobbler
Peach Cobbler
Peach and Blueberry Crisp
Fruit Pizza
Strawberry Cake

Flowered Angel Food Cake
Mississippi Mud Cake
Banana Walnut Cake
Pineapple Upside-Down Cake
Dump Cake
Chocolate Pound Cake with Mexican-
Chocolate Glaze
Chocolate Chip Cake
Strawberry and Cinnamon Coffeecake
Blueberry Sour Cream Coffeecake
Chocolate Zucchini Bundt Cake
Strawberry Chocolate Chip Shortcake
Banana Pudding
Chocolate-Covered Cherry Pudding
Strawberry Banana Sorbet
Ice Cream Sandwiches
Chocolate Chip Biscotti
Chocolate Gingersnaps
Chocolate Raspberry Granola Squares
Berry Patch Bars
Chocolate Mint Brownies
Fat-Free Rice Krispies Treats

A Recommendation for Desserts...

Desserts are the occasional treats included in a healthy eating plan. We've loaded many of these favorites with nutrient-rich fruits and in some cases vegetables. No broccoli, just a little zucchini in a chocolate cake. If having desserts around tempts you to indulge, share half with a friend. Some of the recipes, such as the cobblers and crisps, can be frozen before baking, to be enjoyed at a later time.

Dutch Apple Crumble

A tasty way to keep the doctor away!

5 1/2 c. thinly-sliced apples (~6 apples)
1/3 c. brown sugar, firmly packed
3/4 c. sugar, divided use
1/8 tsp. salt
1/2 tsp. cinnamon, divided use
Nonstick vegetable cooking spray
1/4 c. margarine
1 c. flour
1/4 tsp. baking soda
Nonfat vanilla frozen yogurt (optional)

1. Toss apples with brown sugar, 1/4 cup sugar, salt and 1/4 teaspoon cinnamon.
2. Place into a 9-inch pie pan, that has been coated with cooking spray.
3. Combine margarine, flour, 1/2 cup sugar, baking soda and 1/4 teaspoon cinnamon with pastry blender or in food processor until mixture resembles cornmeal.
4. Sprinkle this mixture over apples, patting lightly with fingers.
5. Bake at 350°F. for 60 minutes. (You may want to place a cookie sheet under the pie pan in case juices boil over.)
6. Allow to cool.
7. Top with nonfat vanilla frozen yogurt, if desired.

Yield: 8 servings
Per Serving:
    249 cal, 6 gm fat, 2 gm pro, 49 gm carb, 0 mg chol,
    129 mg sodium, 2 gm dietary fiber

Pear Raspberry Crumble

A tasty variation of our Dutch Apple Crumble.

3 c. sliced fresh pears
1 (12 oz.) package unsweetened frozen raspberries
2 T. dry tapioca
1/3 c. brown sugar, firmly packed
3/4 c. sugar, divided use
1/8 tsp. salt
1/2 tsp. cinnamon, divided use
Nonstick vegetable cooking spray
1/4 c. margarine
1 c. flour
1/4 tsp. baking soda
Nonfat vanilla frozen yogurt (optional)

1. Toss pears and raspberries with tapioca, brown sugar, 1/4 cup sugar, salt and 1/4 teaspoon cinnamon.
2. Place into 9-inch pie pan, that has been coated with cooking spray.
3. Combine margarine, flour, 1/2 cup sugar, baking soda and 1/4 teaspoon cinnamon with pastry blender or in food processor until mixture resembles cornmeal.
4. Sprinkle this mixture over fruit, patting lightly with fingers.
5. Bake at 350°F. for 60 minutes. (You may want to place a cookie sheet under the pie pan in case juices boil over.)
6. Allow to cool.
7. Top with nonfat vanilla frozen yogurt, if desired.

Yield: 8 servings
Per Serving:
    270 cal, 6 gm fat, 2 gm pro, 54 gm carb, 0 mg chol,
    129 mg sodium, 5 gm dietary fiber

Blueberry and Cream Pie

Blueberries in a cloud.

Pie Crust:
1 1/4 c. graham cracker crumbs
1/4 c. brown sugar, firmly packed
3 T. margarine
1 tsp. grated lemon peel
Nonstick vegetable cooking spray

Filling:
4 c. fresh blueberries, divided use
2 T. cornstarch
2 T. water
1/2 c. light corn syrup
2 tsp. lemon juice
3 oz. Cool Whip Lite

1. Place all crust ingredients in food processor and process until combined.
2. Coat a 9-inch pie plate with cooking spray.
3. Using back of a large spoon, press crumb mixture firmly into bottom and on sides of pie plate.
4. Bake crust at 375°F. for 8 minutes; cool.
5. Place 1 cup blueberries in food processor and process until smooth.
6. Combine cornstarch and water in a medium saucepan, stirring until smooth.
7. Add corn syrup, lemon juice and blueberry puree. Bring to a boil over medium heat, stirring constantly. Allow to boil, while stirring, for 1 minute.
8. Cool for 20 minutes.
9. Fold in remaining 3 cups blueberries.
10. Spread Cool Whip over bottom of pie crust.
11. Spoon blueberry mixture into pie crust on top of Cool Whip. Chill for 2 hours.

Yield: 8 servings
Per Serving:
244 cal, 7 gm fat, 2 gm pro, 43 gm carb, 0 mg chol,
160 mg sodium, 2 gm fiber

Lemon Meringue Pie

A piece of lemon meringue pie can have as many as fourteen grams of fat. This pie lets you indulge with fifty-seven percent less guilt.

Pie Crust:
1 1/4 c. flour
1/4 tsp. salt
1 1/2 T. sugar
4 T. margarine
2 to 4 T. ice-cold water

Filling:
1 (2.9 oz.) box cook & serve lemon pudding mix
2/3 c. sugar, divided use
2 1/4 c. water, divided use
1/4 c. egg substitute
3 egg whites

1. To make crust, place flour, salt, sugar and margarine in a food processor. Pulse for 30 seconds until mixture resembles cornmeal. Continue to pulse, adding ice-cold water, 1 tablespoon at a time, until the mixture just holds together.
2. Form the dough into a disk and place between 2 large pieces of wax paper. Chill in refrigerator for 45 minutes.
3. Roll pie dough into a circle 2 inches larger than pie pan. Line the pan with the dough and crimp the edges.
4. Poke bottom of crust several times with a fork and bake at 375°F. for 15 minutes.
5. In a medium saucepan, stir together pudding mix, 1/3 cup sugar, 1/4 cup water and egg substitute. Add remaining 2 cups water and cook over medium heat, stirring until mixture comes to a full boil. Cool for 5 minutes, stirring twice. Pour into baked pie shell.
6. Beat egg whites until foamy. Gradually beat in remaining 1/3 cup sugar until stiff. Spread over filling and bake at 350°F. for 10 to 15 minutes, until meringue is slightly browned.
7. Cool at room temperature for 4 hours.

Yield: 8 servings
Per Serving:
242 cal, 6 gm fat, 4 gm pro, 44 gm carb, 0 mg chol,
216 mg sodium, 0 gm dietary fiber

Key Lime Pie

Look for bottled Key lime juice to ease the preparation of this summertime favorite.

1 c. water
3/4 c. plus 2 T. sugar, divided use
2 1/2 T. grated lime zest, divided use
1 envelope unflavored gelatin
1/3 c. fresh or bottled Key lime juice
1/4 c. egg substitute
1 1/4 c. graham cracker crumbs
1/4 c. brown sugar, firmly packed
3 T. margarine
Nonstick vegetable cooking spray
2 egg whites
4 oz. (1 3/4 c.) Cool Whip Lite

1. Combine water, 1/2 cup sugar and 1 1/2 tablespoons lime zest in a small saucepan, and simmer for 30 minutes or until reduced to 1/3 to 1/2 cup. Strain and discard zest.
2. Sprinkle gelatin over top and allow to soften for 1 minute. Stir in lime juice, 1/4 cup sugar and egg substitute. Cook over low heat, stirring constantly, until mixture is thick and frothy, about 5 minutes. Allow to cool to room temperature.
3. Place graham cracker crumbs, brown sugar, 1 tablespoon lime zest and margarine in food processor or blender and process until combined.
4. Using a large spoon, press crumb mixture into bottom and sides of a 9-inch pie plate, that has been coated with cooking spray. Bake at 375°F. for 8 minutes; cool.
5. Beat 2 egg whites with remaining 2 tablespoons sugar until stiff. Fold Cool Whip into egg whites, drizzling in reserved lime syrup at the same time. When mixture is smooth, spoon it into crust and chill, uncovered, until firm, about 2 to 3 hours.

Yield: 8 servings
Per Serving:
253 cal, 7 gm fat, 3 gm pro, 43 gm carb, 0 mg chol, 158 mg sodium, 1 gm dietary fiber

French Strawberry Pie

This pie has been passed down through two generations. Currently, this strawberry pie is the reward for homeruns hit by Amanda Kirk. Reward yourself for some homerun you've hit recently!

Pie Crust:
1 1/4 c. flour
1/4 tsp. salt
1 1/2 T. sugar
4 T. margarine
2 to 4 T. ice-cold water

Filling:
2 T. fat-free cream cheese
2 T. reduced-fat cream cheese
4 c. sliced fresh strawberries, divided use
3/4 c. water, divided use
1 c. sugar
4 tsp. cornstarch
1 T. lemon juice
Cool Whip Lite (optional)

1. To make crust, place flour, salt, sugar and margarine in food processor. Pulse for 30 seconds, until mixture resembles cornmeal. Continue to pulse, adding ice-cold water, 1 tablespoon at a time, until the mixture just holds together.
2. Form the dough into a disk and place between 2 large pieces of wax paper. Chill in the refrigerator for 45 minutes.
3. Roll pie dough into a circle 2 inches larger than pie pan. Line the pan with the dough and crimp the edges.
4. Poke bottom of crust several times with a fork and bake at 375°F. for 15 minutes.

Continued on following page.

Continued from preceding page.

5. Combine cream cheese and spread over bottom of baked crust.
6. Top with 1 1/2 cups strawberries.
7. Place 1/2 cup water and 2 1/2 cups strawberries in a saucepan and simmer for 3 minutes.
8. Stir sugar, cornstarch and 1/4 cup water together. Pour into strawberry mixture and bring mixture to a boil. Boil for 1 minute, stirring constantly. Remove from heat and add lemon juice*.
9. Pour strawberry mixture into pie crust and refrigerate for 4 hours.
10. Allow pie to cool and serve with a small amount of Cool Whip Lite, if desired.

*Add a few drops of red food coloring to strawberry mixture if a deeper red color is desired.

Yield: 8 servings
Per Serving:
    274 cal, 7 gm fat, 3 gm pro, 49 gm carb, 3 mg chol,
    166 mg sodium, 2 gm dietary fiber

Very Berry Pie

Folding the crust toward the center gives this pie a hearty look.

Pie Crust:
1 1/2 c. flour
1/4 tsp. salt
1 1/2 T. sugar
5 T. margarine
1/3 to 1/2 c. ice-cold water

Filling:
2 c. fresh raspberries*
2 c. fresh blackberries*
2 c. fresh strawberries*
1 T. lemon juice
1/4 c. flour
2/3 c. sugar
Nonfat vanilla frozen yogurt (optional)

*Can also use unsweetened frozen berries, just defrost and drain first.

1. To make crust, place flour, salt, sugar and margarine in a food processor. Pulse for 30 seconds until mixture resembles cornmeal. Continue to pulse, adding ice-cold water, 1 tablespoon at a time, until the mixture just holds together.
2. Form the dough into a disk and place between 2 large pieces of wax paper. Chill in the refrigerator for 45 minutes.
3. Roll pie dough into a circle 4 inches larger than pie pan. Line pan with dough, allowing excess to hang over the sides.
4. Combine berries with remaining ingredients, excluding topping, and pour into pie shell.
5. Fold excess dough over berries toward pie's center.
6. Bake at 375°F. for 45 to 55 minutes until pastry is lightly browned.
7. Allow pie to cool, and serve with nonfat vanilla frozen yogurt, if desired.

Yield: 8 servings
Per Serving:
272 cal, 8 gm fat, 4 gm pro, 48 gm carb, 0 mg chol,
151 mg sodium, 6 gm dietary fiber

160

Raspberry Pie

Raspberries and a little cinnamon in this one.

Pie Crust:
1 1/2 c. flour
1/4 tsp. salt
1 1/2 T. sugar
5 T. margarine
1/3 to 1/2 c. ice-cold water

Filling:
6 c. fresh raspberries*
1 T. lemon juice
1/4 c. flour
1 c. sugar
1 tsp. cinnamon
Nonfat vanilla frozen yogurt (optional)

*Can also use unsweetened frozen berries, just defrost and drain first.

1. To make crust, place flour, salt, sugar and margarine in a food processor. Pulse for 30 seconds until mixture resembles cornmeal. Continue to pulse, adding ice-cold water, 1 tablespoon at a time, until the mixture just holds together.
2. Form the dough into a disk and place between 2 large pieces of wax paper. Chill in refrigerator for 45 minutes.
3. Roll pie dough into a circle 4 inches larger than pie pan. Line pan with dough, allowing excess to hang over the sides.
4. Combine berries with remaining ingredients, excluding topping, and pour into pie shell.
5. Fold excess dough over berries toward pie's center.
6. Bake at 375°F. for 45 to 55 minutes until pastry is lightly browned.
7. Allow the pie to cool, and serve with nonfat vanilla frozen yogurt, if desired.

Yield: 8 servings
Per Serving:
303 cal, 8 gm fat, 3 gm pro, 57 gm carb, 0 mg chol,
150 mg sodium, 8 gm dietary fiber

Brownie Pie

Go ahead and indulge.

1 (19.85 oz.) box light brownie mix
Nonstick vegetable cooking spray
3 bananas, sliced*
1 pt. strawberries, stem removed & sliced*
4 kiwi, sliced*
1/2 c. chocolate syrup

*Substitute other fruits such as raspberries, cherries, blueberries, etc.

1. Prepare brownie batter according to package directions, using 2 egg whites for 1 egg, if an egg is required. Pour into a 9-inch pie pan, that has been coated with cooking spray.
2. Bake at 350°F. for 40 minutes; allow to cool.
3. When cool, cut into 12 pieces. Place on individual plates and decorate with sliced fruit. Drizzle 2 teaspoons chocolate syrup over each piece and serve.

Yield: 12 servings
Per Serving:
   282 cal, 5 gm fat, 3 gm pro, 58 gm carb, 2 mg chol,
   174 mg sodium, 2 gm dietary fiber

Chocolate Chip and Peppermint Brownie Pie

Make this during the Christmas season, using candy canes for the peppermints.

1 (19.85 oz.) box light brownie mix
Nonstick vegetable cooking spray
1/4 c. chocolate chips
3 T. crushed peppermints

1. Prepare brownie batter according to package directions, using 2 egg whites for 1 egg, if an egg is required. Pour into a 9-inch pie pan, that has been coated with cooking spray.
2. Sprinkle top with chocolate chips and peppermint.
3. Bake at 350°F. for 40 minutes. Allow to cool before cutting into pieces.

Yield: 10 servings
Per Serving:
    279 cal, 6 gm fat, 3 gm pro, 53 gm carb, 0 mg chol,
    203 mg sodium, 0 gm dietary fiber

Strawberry, Blueberry and Raspberry Cobbler

The wholewheat crust makes this cobbler "berry" delicious.

8 c. combination of fresh strawberries, blueberries & raspberries*
10 T. sugar, divided use
1 T. fresh lemon juice
Grated peel of 1/2 lemon
2 T. dry tapioca
1 c. flour
1 c. wholewheat flour
1/8 tsp. salt
1 T. baking powder
1/2 tsp. cinnamon
1/4 c. margarine
1 c. skim milk
Nonfat vanilla frozen yogurt (optional)

*Can also use unsweetened frozen berries.

1. In a large bowl, combine berries with 6 tablespoons sugar, lemon juice, lemon peel and tapioca. Toss well and spoon into a 9x13-inch baking dish.
2. Combine flours, salt, baking powder, cinnamon and remaining 4 tablespoons sugar. Cut margarine into flour mixture, using a pastry blender or food processor, until mixture resembles cornmeal. Stir in skim milk just until blended.
3. Spoon dough over berries and bake at 400°F. for 35 to 45 minutes, until browned.
4. Serve immediately, topping with frozen yogurt, if desired.

Yield: 12 servings
Per Serving:
    199 cal, 5 gm fat, 4 gm pro, 38 gm carb, 0 mg chol,
    181 mg sodium, 5 gm dietary fiber

Peach Cobbler

Oh, the peaches of summer!

5 c. sliced fresh peaches
2/3 c. plus 4 tsp. sugar, divided use
1 T. cornstarch
1 c. water
1 c. flour
1 1/2 tsp. baking powder
1/2 tsp. salt
2 T. margarine
1/2 c. skim milk
1/4 tsp. cinnamon

1. In a large saucepan, combine peaches, 2/3 cup sugar, corn-starch and water. Bring to a boil and boil for 1 minute, stirring constantly.
2. Pour into a 1 1/2-quart baking dish.
3. Combine flour, 3 teaspoons sugar, baking powder, salt and margarine with pastry blender or food processor, until mixture resembles cornmeal.
4. Stir milk into the flour mixture and drop by spoonfuls onto fruit.
5. Combine remaining 1 teaspoon sugar and cinnamon; sprinkle over top.
6. Bake at 400°F. for 25 to 30 minutes, until browned.

Yield: 6 servings
Per Serving:
    276 cal, 4 gm fat, 4 gm pro, 58 gm carb, 0 mg chol,
    334 mg sodium, 3 gm dietary fiber

Peach and Blueberry Crisp

Bake this one in two (nine by nine-inch) pans and share one with a friend or neighbor.

7 c. sliced fresh peaches
3 c. fresh or frozen blueberries
1/3 c. sugar
1/4 c. orange juice
3 T. plus 1/3 c. flour, divided use
1 1/2 c. rolled oats
1/2 c. brown sugar, firmly packed
1 tsp. cinnamon
1/4 tsp. salt
1/4 c. margarine, melted

1. Gently toss peaches and blueberries in sugar, orange juice and 3 tablespoons flour. Pour mixture into a 9x13-inch pan.
2. Stir remaining ingredients together and sprinkle over peaches.
3. Bake at 375°F. for 20 minutes.

Yield: 12 servings
Per Serving:
    214 cal, 5 gm fat, 3 gm pro, 38 gm carb, 0 mg chol,
    95 mg sodium, 4 gm dietary fiber

Fruit Pizza

Match the fresh fruit to the season, yellow and orange fruits in the fall, red and green fruits at Christmas, red and blue fruits on July Fourth.

1 (20 oz.) roll refrigerated sugar cookie dough
1 c. nonfat cottage cheese
1 1/2 T. powdered sugar
1/2 tsp. vanilla extract
4 c. sliced fresh fruit (strawberries, blueberries, kiwi, etc.)
1/2 c. all-fruit apricot jelly

1. Spread sugar cookie dough into a 12- or 13-inch pizza pan, or square pan of similar size.
2. Bake at 350°F. for 10 to 12 minutes until lightly browned.
3. In a food processor, combine cottage cheese, sugar and vanilla; process until smooth.
4. Spread cottage cheese mixture over cooled cookie. Arrange fruit decoratively on top.
5. Melt jelly in microwave (about 30 to 45 seconds) and drizzle over fruit.

Yield: 16 servings
Per Serving:
    211 cal, 7 gm fat, 3 gm pro, 34 gm carb, 1 mg chol,
    212 mg sodium, 2 gm dietary fiber

Strawberry Cake

A beautiful pink cake. See our recipe makeover on this one.

5 oz. plus 3 T. sweetened frozen strawberries, divided use
1 (18 1/4 oz.) box light white cake mix
1 (3 oz.) box strawberry gelatin
1 T. flour
1 1/2 c. water
1 c. egg substitute or 8 egg whites
Nonstick vegetable cooking spray
2 1/2 c. powdered sugar
1/4 tsp. salt
6 T. margarine, softened

1. Defrost strawberries.
2. In a mixing bowl, combine cake mix, gelatin, flour, water, egg substitute or egg whites, and 5 ounces defrosted strawberries with juice. Beat at medium speed for 2 minutes.
3. Pour batter into a 9x13-inch pan, that has been coated with cooking spray.
4. Bake at 350°F. for 30 to 35 minutes, until toothpick inserted in center comes out clean. Allow to cool.
5. Combine powdered sugar, salt, margarine and 3 tablespoons strawberries, without juice, in a mixing bowl, and beat until smooth and creamy. Frost cooled cake.

Yield: 20 servings
Per Serving:
    229 cal, 6 gm fat, 2 gm pro, 42 gm carb, 0 mg chol,
    266 mg sodium, 0 gm dietary fiber

Flowered Angel Food Cake

Serve this in the spring when the flowers are beginning to bloom. Edible flowers can be found in the produce section of your grocery store next to the fresh herbs.

2 c. any combination of unsweetened frozen blueberries, straw-
     berries and/or blackberries*
2 tsp. cornstarch
1/2 tsp. lemon juice
2 T. berry jelly
1 angel food cake
3 c. Cool Whip Lite
1 1/2 c. fresh blueberries, blackberries or strawberries
1 (1/4 oz.) package edible fresh flowers

*Can also use fresh berries; just use 1/3 cup orange juice in place of berry juice.

1.   Defrost frozen berries, reserving juice.
2.   In a saucepan, combine berry juice or orange juice, cornstarch and lemon juice.
3.   Bring mixture to a boil and simmer gently for 1 minute. Stir in jelly until it melts.
4.   Add the defrosted fruit and mash slightly while cooking for another minute. Chill in refrigerator.
5.   Slice angel food cake in half horizontally and place bottom half on serving plate. Spread 1/3 of Cool Whip on bottom half and top with fresh berries, placing several close to the outside edge for decoration.
6.   Top with remaining half of cake and spread remaining Cool Whip over the top, allowing some to go over the edge to decorate top half of cake. Arrange edible flowers and remaining 1/2 cup berries on top of cake. Refrigerate cake.
7.   When ready to serve, spoon berry sauce on plate, making a puddle, and place cake slice in center of puddle.

Yield: 12 servings
Per Serving:
     199 cal, 2 gm fat, 3 gm pro, 39 gm carb, 0 mg chol,
     255 mg sodium, 2 gm dietary fiber

Mississippi Mud Cake

Tastes more like candy than cake.

Cake:
7 T. margarine
1 3/4 c. sugar
1 c. egg substitute or 8 egg whites
1 tsp. vanilla extract
1 1/2 c. flour
1/3 c. cocoa powder
Nonstick vegetable cooking spray
1 (7 oz.) jar marshmallow creme

Frosting:
1/4 c. margarine
1/2 c. skim milk
1/3 c. cocoa powder
1 tsp. vanilla extract
1 (16 oz.) box powdered sugar
1/4 c. chopped pecans

1. With a mixer, cream margarine and sugar together until light and fluffy. Beat in egg substitute or egg whites and vanilla.
2. Add flour and cocoa powder to creamed mixture; mix well.
3. Spread batter into a 9x13-inch pan, that has been coated with cooking spray.
4. Bake at 350°F. for 25 minutes.
5. Remove from oven and immediately spread marshmallow creme over top.
6. In a small saucepan, heat margarine, milk, cocoa powder and vanilla. When margarine is melted, beat in powdered sugar.
7. Spread frosting on hot cake and sprinkle with nuts.

Yield: 24 servings
Per Serving:
      249 cal, 6 gm fat, 2 gm pro, 48 gm carb, 0 mg chol,
      93 mg sodium, 1 gm dietary fiber

Banana Walnut Cake

1 (18 1/4 oz.) box light white cake mix
1/2 c. water
2 bananas, mashed
3 egg whites or 6 T. egg substitute
1/4 c. chopped walnuts
Nonstick vegetable cooking spray
1 (16 oz.) container light white frosting

1. Combine cake mix, water, bananas, and egg whites or egg substitute in a large bowl. Beat on medium speed for 2 minutes.
2. Fold in walnuts.
3. Pour batter into a 9x13-inch pan, that has been coated with cooking spray.
4. Bake at 350°F. for 32 to 37 minutes, until toothpick inserted in center comes out clean. Allow to cool.
5. When cool, spread frosting over top.

Yield: 15 servings
Per Serving:
    278 cal, 5 gm fat, 4 gm pro, 54 gm carb, 0 mg chol,
    290 mg sodium, 0 gm dietary fiber

Pineapple Upside-Down Cake

Nonstick vegetable cooking spray
2 (8 oz.) cans pineapple slices, packed in juice
3/4 c. brown sugar
8 maraschino cherries
1 c. unsweetened applesauce
6 egg whites or 3/4 c. egg substitute
1 (18 1/4 oz.) box light yellow cake mix

1. Coat a 9x13-inch pan with cooking spray. Use a Teflon-coated pan to ensure cake turns out of pan with ease.
2. Drain pineapple, reserving juice.
3. Stir 1/3 cup reserved juice and brown sugar together. Pour into pan. Place 8 slices of pineapple in bottom of pan in 2 rows of 4. Place a cherry in center of each pineapple slice.
4. Combine applesauce, 1/2 cup pineapple juice, egg whites or egg substitute, and cake mix; beat on high for 2 minutes.
5. Pour cake mix over pineapple and bake at 350°F. for 40 to 45 minutes, until toothpick inserted in center comes out clean.
6. Allow to cool for 15 minutes and invert onto a large plate. (If you do not have a plate large enough, place wax paper on counter, invert, and then cut into serving pieces.)

Yield: 12 servings
Per Serving:
    255 cal, 2 gm fat, 4 gm pro, 55 gm carb, 0 mg chol,
    320 mg sodium, 1 gm dietary fiber

Dump Cake

The name says it all. Just a few minutes of dumping and you have a great dessert.

1 (20 oz.) can light cherry pie filling
1 (15 1/4 oz.) can crushed pineapple, packed in juice & drained
1 (18 1/4 oz.) box light yellow cake mix
1 1/2 c. unsweetened applesauce
3 T. chopped pecans
2 T. rolled oats

1. Dump cherry pie filling into a 9x13-inch baking dish; spread over bottom of pan.
2. Dump drained pineapple over cherries.
3. Mix together cake mix and applesauce. Dump over pineapple and spread to cover.
4. Sprinkle top of cake with pecans and oatmeal.
5. Bake at 350°F. for 1 hour.

Yield: 12 servings
Per Serving:
    242 cal, 4 gm fat, 3 gm pro, 52 gm carb, 0 mg chol,
    309 mg sodium, 3 gm dietary fiber

Chocolate Pound Cake with Mexican-Chocolate Glaze

The chocolate-covered almonds that top this cake make it irresistible.

Cake:
1/4 c. margarine
2 1/2 c. sugar
1 1/4 c. egg substitute or 10 egg whites
1 T. vanilla extract
1 c. cocoa powder
2 c. flour
1 T. cinnamon
1/2 tsp. baking powder
1 tsp. salt
1 c. skim milk
1/4 c. water
Nonstick vegetable cooking spray

Glaze:
1/2 c. half & half
3 oz. Mexican chocolate (Ibarra, Abuelita's, La India, or other)
1 oz. bittersweet chocolate
1 T. margarine
1 T. honey
1 T. corn syrup
3 T. whole almonds, toasted*

*To toast almonds, place them under broiler just until lightly browned and fragrant. This takes just a couple of minutes, so watch them carefully!

1. With a mixer, cream margarine and sugar together until light and fluffy. Beat in egg substitute or egg whites, and vanilla extract.

Continued on following page.

Continued from preceding page.

2. In a separate bowl, stir cocoa, flour, cinnamon, baking powder and salt together.
3. In another bowl, combine milk and water.
4. Add 1/3 of milk mixture and 1/3 of flour mixture to creamed mixture and stir together. Repeat this process until all ingredients are combined.
5. Pour batter into a 10-inch bundt pan, that has been coated with cooking spray. Bake for 1 hour at 350°F., or until toothpick inserted into center comes out clean. Allow cake to cool 15 to 20 minutes. Remove cake from pan.
6. To make glaze, place half and half in a small saucepan and heat it on medium for 5 minutes, or until it is slightly scalded; set aside.
7. In the top of a simmering double boiler, place Mexican and bittersweet chocolates, margarine, honey, corn syrup and almonds. Heat until the chocolate and margarine are melted. Stir in scalded half and half and remove pan from heat. Allow to cool for 10 minutes.
8. Spoon glaze over top of cake.

Yield: 20 servings
Per Serving:
    238 cal, 6 gm fat, 4 gm pro, 43 gm carb, 2 mg chol,
    182 mg sodium, 2 gm dietary fiber

Chocolate Chip Cake

A family favorite you can feel good about serving.

Cake:
2 c. flour
1 1/4 c. sugar
2 tsp. baking powder
1/2 tsp. baking soda
1/2 tsp. salt
1 1/2 c. nonfat sour cream
3 T. margarine, softened
1 tsp. vanilla extract
6 egg whites or 3/4 c. egg substitute
Nonstick vegetable cooking spray

Topping:
1 tsp. cinnamon
1/2 c. sugar
1/2 c. chocolate chips

1. Combine all cake ingredients and beat at medium speed for 3 minutes.
2. Pour half of batter into a 9x13-inch pan, that has been coated with cooking spray.
3. For topping, stir cinnamon into sugar. Sprinkle 1/2 this mixture over batter and top with 1/2 the chocolate chips.
4. Pour remaining batter over chocolate chips and sprinkle with remaining sugar mixture and chocolate chips.
5. Bake at 350°F. for 30 to 35 minutes, until toothpick inserted ir center comes out clean.

Yield: 15 servings
Per Serving:
222 cal, 4 gm fat, 4 gm pro, 43 gm carb, 0 mg chol,
240 mg sodium, 1 gm dietary fiber

Strawberry and Cinnamon Coffeecake

Strawberries are a nice addition to this classic coffeecake.

Cake:
5 T. margarine, softened
1 1/2 c. sugar
4 egg whites or 1/2 c. egg substitute
1 c. nonfat sour cream
1 tsp. vanilla extract
2 c. flour
1 tsp. baking powder
3/4 tsp. salt
Nonstick vegetable cooking spray

Topping:
1 c. sliced fresh strawberries
1 tsp. cinnamon
4 tsp. brown sugar, firmly packed

1. With a mixer, cream margarine and sugar together until light and fluffy. Beat in egg whites or egg substitute.
2. Fold in sour cream and vanilla.
3. In a separate bowl, stir flour, baking powder and salt together.
4. Stir flour mixture into creamed mixture, just until flour is moistened.
5. Pour 1/3 batter into a 10-inch bundt pan, that has been coated with cooking spray. Top with strawberries.
6. Combine remaining topping ingredients and sprinkle 3/4 of this over strawberries.
7. Pour remaining batter into pan and sprinkle with remaining topping mixture.
8. Bake at 350°F. for 55 minutes, or until toothpick inserted in center comes out clean.
9. Allow to cool for 15 to 20 minutes and then remove from pan.

Yield: 16 servings
Per Serving:
      180 cal, 4 gm fat, 3 gm pro, 34 gm carb, 0 mg chol,
      200 mg sodium, 1 gm dietary fiber

Blueberry Sour Cream Coffeecake

A lot of bang for your blueberries.

Cake:
1/2 c. margarine
1 1/2 c. sugar
8 egg whites or 1 c. egg substitute
2 c. nonfat sour cream
4 c. flour
2 tsp. baking soda
1 tsp. salt
Nonstick vegetable cooking spray

Topping:
1/2 c. sugar
2 tsp. cinnamon
2 tsp. vanilla extract
2 c. fresh blueberries
1/3 c. chopped walnuts

1. With a mixer, cream margarine and sugar together until light and fluffy. Beat in egg whites or egg substitute.
2. Fold in sour cream.
3. In a separate bowl, stir flour, baking soda and salt together.
4. Stir flour mixture into creamed mixture, just until flour is moistened.
5. Pour 1/2 of batter into a 10-inch bundt pan, that has been coated with cooking spray.
6. Combine all topping ingredients, except blueberries and nuts. Sprinkle half each of topping mixture, blueberries and nuts over batter in pan.
7. Pour remaining batter into pan and spread to cover topping.
8. Sprinkle with remaining topping mixture, blueberries and walnuts.
9. Bake at 350°F. for 50 to 60 minutes, until toothpick inserted in center comes out clean.
10. Allow to cool for 15 to 20 minutes and then remove from pan.

Yield: 24 servings
Per Serving:
    208 cal, 5 gm fat, 5 gm pro, 37 gm carb, 0 mg chol,
    243 mg sodium, 1 gm dietary fiber

Chocolate Zucchini Bundt Cake

Similar to a coffeecake, works well as a lunch or brunch dessert.

3 T. margarine
2 c. sugar
3 (1 oz.) squares unsweetened baking chocolate, melted & cooled
6 egg whites or 3/4 c. egg substitute
1/2 c. skim milk
2 tsp. vanilla extract
2 c. grated zucchini
2 1/2 c. flour
2 1/2 tsp. baking powder
1 1/2 tsp. baking soda
1/2 tsp. salt
1 1/2 tsp. cinnamon, divided use
Nonstick vegetable cooking spray
2 T. powdered sugar

1. With a mixer, cream margarine and sugar together until light and fluffy. Beat in chocolate, and egg whites or egg substitute.
2. Beat in milk and vanilla extract.
3. Fold in zucchini.
4. In a separate bowl, combine flour, baking powder, baking soda, salt and 1 teaspoon cinnamon.
5. Add flour mixture to creamed mixture; mix well.
6. Pour batter into a 10-inch bundt pan, that has been coated with cooking spray.
7. Bake at 350°F. for 50 minutes, or until toothpick inserted in center comes out clean. Allow to cool for 15 to 20 minutes and then remove from pan.
8. Combine remaining 1/2 teaspoon cinnamon and powdered sugar; sift over cooled cake.

Yield: 20 servings
Per Serving:
    173 cal, 4 gm fat, 3 gm pro, 34 gm carb, 0 mg chol,
    201 mg sodium, 1 gm dietary fiber

Strawberry Chocolate Chip Shortcake

2 1/4 c. reduced-fat Bisquick
2/3 c. skim milk
3 T. sugar
1 1/2 T. margarine, melted
Nonstick vegetable cooking spray
3 T. chocolate chips
1 qt. strawberries, sliced
1 c. Cool Whip Lite

1. Combine Bisquick, milk, sugar and margarine. Mix until soft dough forms.
2. Coat a 9x9-inch baking dish or cookie sheet with cooking spray. Spread batter into baking dish or drop by spoonfuls onto cookie sheet (making 8 shortcakes).
3. Sprinkle top of shortcake with chocolate chips.
4. Bake at 425°F. for 8 to 11 minutes or until golden brown. Cool for 10 minutes.
5. Cut shortcake into 8 pieces if baked in 1 piece. Top each with 1/2 cup strawberries and 2 tablespoons Cool Whip Lite.

Yield: 8 servings
Per Serving:
 228 cal, 7 gm fat, 4 gm pro, 38 gm carb, 0 mg chol,
 419 mg sodium, 2 gm dietary fiber

Banana Pudding

If you can locate sugar-free instant banana pudding mix, use it in place of the vanilla one here and leave out the banana extract.

1 (.9 oz.) box sugar-free instant vanilla pudding mix
2 c. skim milk
1/2 tsp. banana extract
1 c. Cool Whip Lite
2 bananas, sliced
24 vanilla wafers, divided use

1. Combine pudding mix with skim milk and banana extract. Beat with a wire whisk or electric beater on low speed for 1 to 2 minutes until blended. Refrigerate for 2 minutes.
2. Fold in Cool Whip.
3. Line the bottom of 6 custard cups or small bowls with banana slices and 18 of the vanilla wafers.
4. Fill with pudding and top each with a vanilla wafer. Chill until set.

Yield: 6 servings
Per Serving:
    172 cal, 4 gm fat, 4 gm pro, 30 gm carb, 13 mg chol,
    293 mg sodium, 1 gm dietary fiber

Chocolate-Covered Cherry Pudding

Easy, Easy, Easy...

1 (16 oz.) can cherries in water
1 (1 1/2 oz.) box sugar-free instant chocolate fudge pudding mix
4 oz. Cool Whip Lite

1. Mix cherries with liquid and pudding mix together.
2. Fold in Cool Whip and serve.

Yield: 6 servings
Per Serving:
    78 cal, 2 gm fat, 0 gm pro, 14 gm carb, 0 mg chol,
    235 mg sodium, 1 gm dietary fiber

Strawberry Banana Sorbet

3 c. strawberries, stems removed
1 banana
1/2 c. sugar
1/4 c. lemon juice

1. Place all ingredients in a food processor or blender and process until smooth.
2. Place mixture in an ice cream machine and freeze according to manufacturer's directions.

Yield: 5 servings
Per Serving (1/2 cup):
    124 cal, 0 gm fat, 1 gm pro, 31 gm carb, 0 mg chol,
    1 mg sodium, 3 gm dietary fiber

Ice Cream Sandwiches

1 (20 oz.) roll reduced-fat chocolate chip cookie dough
3 3/4 c. nonfat vanilla frozen yogurt

1. Slice roll of cookie dough into 30 pieces and bake according to package directions; allow cookies to cool.
2. When cool, place 1/4 cup yogurt on a cookie. Top with another cookie, pressing down lightly to spread yogurt to edges.
3. Wrap in plastic wrap and freeze for 1 hour, or until ready to eat.

Yield: 15 servings
Per Serving (1 ice cream sandwich):
    198 cal, 5 gm fat, 4 gm pro, 33 gm carb, 5 mg chol,
    152 mg sodium, 1 gm dietary fiber

Chocolate Chip Biscotti

Grab a cup of coffee and enjoy this twice-baked Italian cookie.

2 T. margarine, at room temperature
1/2 c. brown sugar, firmly packed
1/2 c. sugar
4 egg whites or 1/2 c. egg substitute
2 c. flour
1 1/2 tsp. baking powder
1 tsp. cinnamon
1/4 tsp. salt
1/2 c. chocolate chips
Nonstick vegetable cooking spray

1. With a mixer, cream together margarine and both sugars until light and fluffy. Beat in egg whites or egg substitute.
2. In a separate bowl, stir flour, baking powder, cinnamon and salt together. On low speed, mix in the flour mixture, just until incorporated. Stir in the chocolate chips.
3. Divide the dough in half and place on a cookie sheet, that has been coated with cooking spray. Form each half into a log, 3 inches wide by 3/4-inch high.
4. Bake at 325°F. until firm to the touch, about 25 minutes. Remove from oven and let cool for 5 minutes.
5. Using a spatula, transfer logs to a cutting board. Cut logs into 1/2-inch slices, using a serrated knife. Arrange the slices, cut-side down, on cookie sheet.
6. Bake at 325°F. for 10 minutes. Remove from oven. Turn over and bake an additional 10 minutes.
7. Transfer to a cooling rack and store in an airtight container.

Yield: 24 cookies
Per Serving (1 cookie):
    100 cal, 2 gm fat, 2 gm pro, 19 gm carb, 0 mg chol,
    68 mg sodium, 0 gm dietary fiber

Chocolate Gingersnaps

Chewy and Chocolatey!

1/3 c. margarine
1 1/4 c. sugar, divided use
2 egg whites or 1/4 c. egg substitute
1/4 c. molasses
2 c. flour
1/4 c. cocoa powder
1 1/2 tsp. baking soda
2 1/2 tsp. ground ginger
1/2 tsp. salt
Nonstick vegetable cooking spray

1. With a mixer, cream margarine. Gradually add 1 cup sugar, beating at medium speed until light and fluffy.
2. Add egg whites or egg substitute; beat well.
3. Stir in molasses.
4. In a separate bowl, stir flour, cocoa powder, baking soda, ginger and salt together. Add to creamed mixture, stirring well.
5. Shape dough into 1-inch balls. Roll in 1/4 cup sugar. Place 2 inches apart on cookie sheets coated with cooking spray.
6. Bake at 350°F. for 10 to 12 minutes. Cool completely.

Yield: 48 cookies
Per Serving (1 cookie):
     53 cal, 1 gm fat, 1 gm pro, 10 gm carb, 0 mg chol,
     67 mg sodium, 0 gm dietary fiber

Chocolate Raspberry Granola Squares

1/3 c. chocolate chips
2/3 c. all-fruit raspberry jam
2 1/2 c. low-fat granola
1 tsp. almond extract
Nonfat vegetable cooking spray

1. In a small saucepan, melt chocolate chips and jam over low heat, stirring constantly.
2. Remove from heat and stir in granola and almond extract.
3. Spread mixture into a 9x9-inch pan, that has been coated with cooking spray.
4. Refrigerate for 1 hour or until firm. Cut into 12 squares.

Yield: 12 servings
Per Servings (1 square):
   152 cal, 3 gm fat, 2 gm pro, 30 gm carb, 0 mg chol,
   52 mg sodium, 1 gm dietary fiber

Berry Patch Bars

Good treat to put in the kids' lunches.

1/3 c. margarine
1/2 c. sugar
1 tsp. vanilla extract
2 egg whites or 1/4 c. egg substitute
2 1/2 c. flour
1/2 tsp. baking powder
1/8 tsp. salt
Nonstick vegetable cooking spray
20 oz. (~2 c.) all-fruit raspberry, strawberry, or other berry jam
2 T. powdered sugar

1. With a mixer, cream together margarine and sugar. Add vanilla, and egg whites or egg substitute; beat well.
2. Stir together flour, baking powder and salt; gradually stir into creamed mixture, mixing well after each addition. Dough will be crumbly.
3. Press dough lightly over bottom and sides of a 9x13-inch baking dish, that has been coated with cooking spray.
4. Bake at 375°F. for 15 to 20 minutes, until just lightly browned around edges. Do not overbake.
5. Heat jam in a saucepan. When melted, spread over cookie dough.
6. Allow to cool for 20 to 30 minutes and then sift powdered sugar over top. Store in refrigerator.

Yield: 40 bars
Per Serving (1 bar):
  90 cal, 2 gm fat, 1 gm pro, 18 gm carb, 0 mg chol,
  32 mg sodium, 0 gm dietary fiber

Chocolate Mint Brownies

Brownies with frosting, and only two grams of fat each!

Brownies:
3/4 c. sugar
2 T. margarine, melted
3/4 c. egg substitute or 6 egg whites
1 c. flour
1/2 tsp. salt
1 (16 oz.) can chocolate syrup
Nonstick vegetable cooking spray

Frosting:
2 c. powdered sugar
2 T. margarine, melted
1/2 tsp. peppermint extract
2 T. skim milk
Few drops of green food coloring

1. Stir all brownie ingredients together just until moistened. Pour into a 9x13-inch pan, that has been coated with cooking spray.
2. Bake at 350°F. for 30 minutes; allow to cool.
3. Combine frosting ingredients and spread over cooled brownies.

Yield: 24 brownies
Per Serving (1 brownie):
    145 cal, 2 gm fat, 2 gm pro, 31 gm carb, 0 mg chol,
    99 mg sodium, 0 gm dietary fiber

Fat-Free Rice Krispies Treats

No secret here, just leave the margarine out of the original recipe.

Nonstick vegetable cooking spray
1 (10 oz.) package marshmallows
6 c. Rice Krispies cereal

1. Place marshmallows in a large saucepan, that has been coated with cooking spray.
2. Heat until marshmallows are completely melted, stirring constantly.
3. Remove from heat and stir in cereal.
4. Press mixture into a 9x13-inch pan, that has been coated with cooking spray.
5. When cool, cut into squares.

Yield: 24 squares
Per Serving (1 square):
    66 cal, 0 gm fat, 1 gm pro, 16 gm carb, 0 mg chol,
    91 mg sodium, 0 gm dietary fiber

Gifts

Strawberry Freezer Jam

Mulling Spice

Herbs de Provence

Penny's Peppery Zest

Dutch Apple Crumble as a Gift

Hot Fudge Pudding Cake as a Gift

Strawberry Freezer Jam

No butter needed on hot bread with this incredible jam.

20 oz. unsweetened frozen strawberries
3 c. sugar
3 oz. fruit pectin

1. Defrost strawberries and drain liquid.
2. Place strawberries in a bowl and mash a little. Add sugar and let stand 20 minutes, stirring occasionally.
3. Add fruit pectin and stir continuously for 2 minutes.
4. Pour into containers and freeze.

Yield: 4 cups
Per Serving (1 tablespoon):
    38 cal, 0 gm fat, 0 gm pro, 10 gm carb, 0 mg chol,
    0 mg sodium, 0 gm dietary fiber

Mulling Spice

Give to a friend to use in Christmas Cranberry Cider for a no-cal holiday food gift.

2 T. chopped cinnamon sticks
2 T. chopped dried orange peel
2 T. whole cloves
2 T. whole allspice

1. Combine all ingredients and place in an airtight container. Makes 1/2 cup, enough to flavor 96 cups of juice.

Mulling spices are used to flavor juices and are removed before serving.

No nutritional analysis needed on this one.

⸮ Provence

*wonderful French blend of herbs, used in our
la Cheese and Herbed Pork Tenderloin with
lustard Sauce recipes.*

osemary
basil
. fennel seed
yme
.vender*
∴ sage
T. summer savory
, T. marjoram

)mit the lavender if you have difficulty locating it. It will still be
ι wonderful herb blend.

1. Combine all herbs and place in a decorative container.

Yield: 1/2 cup
Per Serving (1 teaspoon):
5 cal, 0 gm fat, 0 gm pro, 1 gm carb, 0 mg chol,
1 mg sodium, 0 gm dietary fiber

Penny's Peppery Zest

This is a spicy seasoning to rub into chicken.

2 tsp. onion powder
2 tsp. garlic powder
2 tsp. paprika
1 tsp. chili powder
1/2 tsp. cayenne pepper
1/2 tsp. seasoned pepper
1/2 tsp. curry powder
1/2 tsp. lemon pepper
1/2 tsp. white pepper
1/2 tsp. black pepper

1. Combine all seasonings and place in a small spice container.

Yield: 10 teaspoons
Per Serving (1 teaspoon):
    8 cal, 0 gm fat, 0 gm pro, 1 gm carb, 0 mg chol,
    20 mg sodium, 0 gm dietary fiber

Dutch Apple Crumble as a Gift

1/3 c. brown sugar, firmly packed
3/4 c. sugar, divided use
1/8 tsp. salt
1/2 tsp. cinnamon, divided use
1 c. flour
1/4 tsp. baking soda
1 (1 c.) container or bag
1 (2 c.) container or bag
6 apples
1 pastry blender (optional)
1 (9-inch) pie plate
1 decorative kitchen towel

1. Combine brown sugar, 1/4 cup sugar, salt and 1/4 teaspoon cinnamon; place into small container or bag.
2. Combine flour, 1/2 cup sugar, baking soda and 1/4 teaspoon cinnamon; place into larger container or bag.
3. Arrange 2 containers/bags, apples, pastry blender and recipe at right in pie plate. Tie towel over middle, allowing ingredients to show.

Dutch Apple Crumble

Dutch Apple Crumble Kit
Nonstick vegetable cooking spray
1/4 c. margarine
Nonfat vanilla frozen yogurt (optional)

1. Toss apples with ingredients in small container.
2. Place into pie pan that has been coated with cooking spray.
3. Cut margarine into ingredients in larger container until mixture resembles cornmeal, using a pastry blender or food processor.
4. Sprinkle this mixture over apples, patting lightly with fingers.
5. Bake at 350°F. for 60 minutes. (You may want to place a cookie sheet under the pie pan in case juices boil over.)
6. Allow to cool.
7. Top with nonfat vanilla frozen yogurt, if desired.

Yield: 8 servings
Per Serving:
   249 cal, 6 gm fat, 2 gm pro, 49 gm carb, 0 mg chol, 129 mg sodium, 2 gm dietary fiber

Recipe from: *More of What's Cooking*

Hot Fudge Pudding Cake as a Gift

A favorite dessert from the first cookbook.

1 1/4 c. sugar, divided use
1 c. flour
7 T. cocoa powder, divided use
2 tsp. baking powder
1/4 tsp. salt
1/2 c. brown sugar, firmly packed
1 (2 c.) bag or container
1 (1 1/2 c.) bag or container
1 decorative container or basket

1. In a medium bowl, combine 3/4 cup sugar, flour, 3 tablespoons cocoa powder, baking powder and salt. Pour into larger bag or container.
2. In a small bowl, combine remaining 1/2 cup sugar, brown sugar and remaining 4 tablespoons cocoa powder. Pour into smaller bag or container.
3. Place both bags in a decorative container or basket and attach recipe at right.

Hot Fudge Pudding Cake

1 Hot Fudge Pudding Cake Kit
1/2 c. skim milk
1/3 c. margarine, melted
1/2 tsp. vanilla extract
1 1/4 c. hot water
Cool Whip Lite (optional)

1. Pour contents of larger bag into a bowl. Blend in skim milk, margarine and vanilla extract; beat until smooth.
2. Pour batter into a 9x9-inch pan.
3. Sprinkle mixture of smaller bag evenly over batter.
4. Pour hot water over top; do not stir.
5. Bake at 350°F. for 40 minutes, or until center is almost set.
6. Let stand 15 minutes.
7. Spoon into dessert dishes, spooning sauce from bottom of pan over top.
8. Garnish with Cool Whip Lite, if desired.

Yield: 9 servings
Per Serving:
276 cal, 7 gm fat, 2 gm pro, 52 gm carb, 0 mg chol, 258 mg sodium, 2 gm dietary fiber

Notes & Recipes

Index

Order Form

More of What's Cooking

More of What's Cooking

Apples to Zucchini, Inc., P.O. Box 25456
Dallas, TX 75225

Please send me_____copies of **More of What's Cooking** at $14.95 plus $3.75 shipping/handling for each book. Texas residents add $1.54 tax. Enclosed is my check for $_____. (Make checks payable to "**Apples to Zucchini, Inc.**")

Name _____

Address _____

City _____ State _____ Zip _____

More of What's Cooking

Apples to Zucchini, Inc., P.O. Box 25456
Dallas, TX 75225

Please send me_____copies of **More of What's Cooking** at $14.95 plus $3.75 shipping/handling for each book. Texas residents add $1.54 tax. Enclosed is my check for $_____. (Make checks payable to "**Apples to Zucchini, Inc.**")

Name _____

Address _____

City _____ State _____ Zip _____

For credit card orders, phone or fax order to
Apples to Zucchini, Inc. at 214-521-7524

Chili-Chicken Tortilla Soup

1 Tbs EVO
1/2 C chopped onion
2 Garlic cloves, minced
4 cups chicken broth
15 oz can of pinto beans, drained
14 1/2 oz chopped tomatoes
1 C chopped chicken
2 fresh Anaheim chili peppers, diced
   (or 1 can of chopped chili peppers)

1 tsp ground cumin
1 tsp chili powder
1/2 tsp oregano
1/2 tsp salt
1/8 tsp pepper
Tortilla chips, green onions (optional)

- Saute onion & garlic in EVO. Add
  broth, beans, tomatoes, chicken, chili
  peppers and seasoning spices.

- Bring to boil, then reduce heat, cover
  and simmer 20-25 mins.

- Laddle into bowls, sprinkle with
  tortilla strips & onions.
  (Makes 6-8 servings)

Order Form

What's Cooking at the Cooper Clinic

What's Cooking at the Cooper Clinic

It's Cooking, Inc., P.O. Box 25456
Dallas, TX 75225

Please send me_____copies of **What's Cooking at the Cooper Clinic** at $14.95 plus $3.75 shipping/handling for each book. Texas residents add $1.54 tax. Enclosed is my check for $_____. (Make checks payable to "**It's Cooking, Inc.**")

Name _____

Address _____

City _____ State _____ Zip _____

What's Cooking at the Cooper Clinic

It's Cooking, Inc., P.O. Box 25456
Dallas, TX 75225

Please send me_____copies of **What's Cooking at the Cooper Clinic** at $14.95 plus $3.75 shipping/handling for each book. Texas residents add $1.54 tax. Enclosed is my check for $_____. (Make checks payable to "**It's Cooking, Inc.**")

Name _____

Address _____

City _____ State _____ Zip _____

For credit card orders, phone or fax order to
It's Cooking, Inc. at 214-521-7524